The Commodity Futures Market From an Agricultural Producer's Point of View

By
T. M. Hammonds

Oregon State University

MSS Information Corporation
655 Madison Avenue, New York, N.Y. 10021

Library of Congress Cataloging in Publication Data

Hammonds, T   M
    The commodity futures market from an agricultural
producer's point of view.

    Bibliography: p.
    1. Commodity exchanges. I. Title.
HG6046.H34   332.6'328   72-86269
ISBN 0-8422-5024-7
ISBN 0-8422-0252-8 (pbk.)

CONTENTS

INTRODUCTION   5

1 *The Nature and Origin of the Commodity Futures*   7
   Market

   The origin of the market . The Speculator . The Basis
   Hedging . Producer Speculation . Market Information

2 *A Few Essential Details*   25

   Short Selling . The Margin Account . Reading Published
   Price Reports

3 *The Trading Process*   34

   Financial Leverage . Types of Orders . Stocks Versus
   Commodities

4 *Traders and Their Objectives*   41

   Hedgers . Speculators . Producer Objectives

5 *Trading Techniques for Producers*   49

   A Pre-Harvest Hedge . A Storage Hedge . Futures Market
   Delivery . Producer Speculation . Hedging Future
   Inventory Requirements . Potential Problems . Inverted
   Markets

6 *Market Analysis*   59

   The First Step . Fundamental Versus Technical Analysis
   . Account Analysis and Trading Techniques . Trading
   Rules

   APPENDIX   68

   SUGGESTED FURTHER READINGS   77

   GLOSSARY   78

   INDEX   86

INTRODUCTION

This book was written to introduce agricultural producers to the Commodity Futures Market. It is deliberately simplified and assumes no previous knowledge of this market.

I have used a preliminary copy of this material in a series of workshops involving over 100 producers and in the college classroom with over 200 students. Their valuable questions and requests for clarification have been integrated into this volume. The futures market is not a simple beast, but experience with this material has shown that anyone can master its workings with a little diligence.

The text can stand on its own, but it was designed for presentation and discussion by a qualified leader. Producer workshops in Oregon are organized as follows: County extension agents are trained as group leaders in a concentrated two-day meeting. These agents then organize producer groups ranging in size from 20 to 30 people in their respective counties. A one-day kick-off meeting is held at which I present the material in Chapters 1 and 2. A slide presentation has been developed to cover Chapter 1 in an entertaining manner. Each remaining chapter is discussed at one of four biweekly county meetings led by the local agent. A paper trading exercise is integrated into the entire program with the extension agent acting as broker. This exercise is extremely valuable and should not be omitted in a course of this type. Anyone organizing a long-term workshop around this text should consider introducing some material on charting from Chapter 6 early in the presentation. This gives the participants a chance to use bar graphs as an aid in their paper trading. For concentrated sessions, charting material should be discussed last.

Historically, producers have not been widespread users of commodity futures. To be sure, a large number of producers do use this market, but this number is a small percentage of all producers. This is ironic because much of the early development of this market took place with producers in mind. All surveys to discover the reason that the percentage of users is low have concluded that very few producers understand this market. It is my belief that the material generally available to producers on futures trading is needlessly complex and often written from a speculator's point of view. I hope that this text suffers from neither of these faults.

Timothy M. Hammonds
Corvallis, Oregon

1

The Nature and Origin of the Commodity Futures Market

The commodity futures market is a complex and highly specialized market. The best way to understand such a market is to examine its operations in terms of the basic functions which must be performed in any marketplace. We can look at these functions one at a time and see how each piece relates to the producer.

The first and best-known function that comes to mind when we think of a market is the physical exchange process: the actual buying and selling of products. In fact, we often define a market as two or more individuals engaged in the exchange process. But there is more to marketing a product than its simple exchange.

In order to bring a product into position for exchange, transportation and storage are needed. These functions are most readily noticed in times of crisis. For example, the 1970-71 dock strike in the Pacific Northwest made everyone painfully aware of the consequences following any disruption of a transportation and storage system. These two functions are considered together because commodity transit is one form of commodity storage. Grain being transported by ship from the West Coast to Japan is an excellent example. When transport facilities become inoperative, alternative storage facilities are often insufficient to handle the total crop volume.

In order to facilitate the transportation and exchange process, we have standardized grading procedures. Grades and standards make price quotations more specific and, therefore, more meaningful, which generally speeds communication between buyer and seller. This function is vital for the commodity futures market. It allows traders to buy and sell commodities without the troublesome and time-consuming necessity of personally inspecting each lot.

Along with the transfer of commodity ownership goes risk. In agricultural trade, there is the possibility of price fluctuation, as well as the possibility of quality deterioration. This double risk can make trading in agricultural products a very hazardous occupation. This fact of life has been the single most important impetus to the development of a futures market. We will return to the problems of risk management several times in the discussion which follows.

The final function which needs to be considered is market information. This may be the simple communication of a price and a quantity between a single buyer and a single seller, or it may be a highly complex reporting system, nationally syndicated through the news media. The more rapid the price movement in a market, the greater the necessity for reliable, current price and movement information. Additional functions may be performed in certain markets, but these basic six must always be present in some form.

The important thing to realize about these functions is that they cannot be eliminated. For example, a farmer selling a random assortment of fruits and vegetables at his roadside stand has not eliminated the grading function. He has merely transferred the burden of determining acceptable quality to the buyer. Neither has he eliminated any transportation. The buyer becomes his own custom hauler. In general, the producer is responsible for each and every one of the functions listed. He is responsible unless, that is, he can find someone outside the production sector willing to assume one or more of these functions in his place and unles, in addition, he can find a mechanism for making the transfer of that function. It is the transfer of these functions, risk in particular, that the futures market accomplishes. If we can monitor these transfers, we can understand the workings of the commodity futures market.

The Origin of the Market

The origin of this market can be most readily under-stood by looking first at the transportation function. Once a purchase has been made and the product is on its way, the new owner traditionally assumes any price risk during ship-ment. This risk is certainly very significant today, as transportation strikes so vividly illustrate, but it was even more significant during the developmental stages of our transportation networks. During the early 1800's, for example, most transportation facilities were slow and cumber-some. Not only was the risk of quality deterioration great with these early facilities, but the time required for tran-sit was longer, making the risk of price fluctuation very large. In addition, communications were also poor, making it difficult to determine the precise location and condition

8

of the shipments before arrival.

If you were a buyer under these conditions, how might you transfer this considerable price risk during product shipment? One method that became popular during the early 1800's was the "To Arrive" contract. The owner of a commodity in transit sold the right of ownership to that product, with the physical transfer of ownership delayed until the product arrived. In this manner, he could establish a firm price in advance of arrival and transfer at least the risk of a market price change to a new owner. Whether or not he maintained the risk of quality deterioration during shipment was subject to negotiation.

A modern equivalent of the "To Arrive" contract is contract production. Many agricultural products, broilers, for example, are currently produced under a firm contract price which is established before delivery is actually made. As we can see, "To Arrive" contracting has been extended to cover products still in the production stage, as well as products in shipment. In this type of transaction, the risk of price fluctuation between the time of price fixing and the time of actual marketing is transferred to a new owner. The price received may not be the best price that prevails during the marketing period, but at least an acceptable price level is guaranteed.

If all agricultural products were sold in this manner, there would be no need for a commodity futures market. But "To Arrive" contracting has its own special problems which tend to limit its usefulness.

First, the producer must search for an individual buyer willing to enter into such a contract with him. This may be a very difficult and time-consuming process. Although arrangements may become well established over the years, with the same parties contracting year after year, the initial contacts are often very difficult to make. It is not unusual for a producer to find no one willing to forward price his product.

Second, the prices negotiated in these contracts are typically not public knowledge. The producer's profit then becomes a function of not only his productive efficiency, but of his individual bargaining skill as well. In this bargaining process, the producer will often be at a disadvantage. He will often be forced to deal with a large-volume buyer who has much better access to market information and current price levels than he does.

Third, there is typically no formal mechanism for settling disputes with this type of contract. For example, a producer may find that if the market price has fallen substantially below the contract price, his product is no longer "in grade" as far as the buyer is concerned. Each party, of course, has access to the courts should the other party default. But this is an expensive and time-consuming process.

We have seen that producers can avoid price risk by transferring that risk on an individual, contractual basis. But this method of transfer may be a difficult and cumbersome process for them to use. In many markets this method will not even be a workable alternative.

The difficulties just described were keenly felt during the early 1800's when "To Arrive" contracting was gaining popularity. In response to these difficulties, the first Commodity Exchange opened in the middle 1800's. Its primary function, at that time, was to facilitate "To Arrive" trading. It did so initially by providing a central meeting place for buyer and seller to congregate. This made the individual search process easier for both parties.

Within a few years, the Exchange performed another facilitating function. The individual negotiated and unique "To Arrive" contracts were standardized for each commodity. Each contract became identical with all others for the same product. In other words, there was now one contract form for each commodity being traded. This eliminated the need for bargaining on an individual basis each time a new trade was to be made. In addition, the standardized nature of each contract made settlement of disputes as orderly and easy as possible. Trading in these standardized contracts became the commodity futures market as we know it today. This market, therefore, grew out of the natural need of cash market dealers to transfer price risk in an easy and efficient manner.

The Commodity Contract

Each commodity futures contract specifies at a minimum the product to be traded, the quantity to be represented by each contract, the quality deliverable under that contract, the acceptable delivery point or points, and, finally, the delivery date at which time each contract expires. Each contract has a limited life, usually less than one year, after which it matures for delivery and then ceases to exist.

It is easiest to think of each contract as a promise to deliver. A seller has promised to make delivery and a buyer has promised to accept that delivery. Once a party has entered into one of these contracts, he has a choice of two methods for fulfilling his contractual obligation. He may actually deliver the physical commodity. Many people, especially producers, think of this as the only method of satisfying the contract. But there is another, and it is this second alternative which makes the futures market unique. He may satisfy his obligation by making an offsetting trade before the contract expiration date. For example, once an individual has purchased a promise to deliver, which is all that a commodity futures contract is, he may sell this promise to someone else. This takes him out of the market before actual delivery time. If he had originally sold a promise to deliver, he could buy it back at any time before the contract expiration date.

Fewer than 1 percent of all futures contracts are settled by delivery. More than 99 percent are settled by this method of making an offsetting trade. Since offsetting trades are so important, let's look at them more closely.

To make this process as easy as possible, the Commodity Exchange maintains a Commodity Clearing House whose job it is to supervise and record all trades. Figure 1 shows three individuals whose accounts would pass through the Clearing House.

Figure I.

11

Individual A, whom we will assume to be a producer, decides that he would like to transfer the price risk while he still holds his commodity. Perhaps he would like to set his price at today's level, but the crop is still growing and cannot be disposed of on the cash market. He, therefore, sells a promise to deliver to Individual B. B has promised to accept A's delivery when he buys the contract. B holds this promise for a period of time and then sells A's promise to deliver to Individual C. If he sells at a higher price than he paid when he originally acquired it, he makes a profit. If price has declined, he experiences a loss. In either case, A is still entitled to the original purchase price and neither gains, nor loses, from any subsequent price fluctuation. The Clearing House records would show that B had purchased a promise to deliver and had later sold it to someone else. B's net position in the futures market is now zero, and he need not take part in the delivery process.[1]

We have seen how one individual out of the 99 percent who never take part in actual delivery operates. Now, let's look at the delivery mechanism. Here we have our same

Figure 2.

---

individuals A, B, and C, but we have added one more and we have also added the Clearing House. A has sold a promise to deliver to B, who has, in turn, sold it to C, leaving B with no net outstanding obligation. Individual C has held A's promise to deliver for a period of time, either making a profit or loss depending on the price fluctuation, and has finally sold it to individual D. Now, Individual C has bought a promise to deliver, and he has resold that promise to deliver, his net position in the market is zero. Individual C has joined the 99 percent of the traders who never take part in the delivery process. Many individuals like B and C should be shown, but only two are included here for purposes of simplification.

Now, let's assume the contract expiration date has arrived. Individual A still has outstanding a promise to deliver. He has not repurchased it because he has decided to become part of the 1 percent who fulfill their contractual obligation by actually making delivery. A gives notice to the Commodity Clearing House and transports his product to a contract-designated warehouse. The Clearing House then gives notice of delivery to Individual D, who is still holding the promise to deliver. D comes to the appropriate warehouse and picks up the product. D and A never have any direct contact with each other; their dealings are entirely through the Clearing House. In fact, none of the people involved would ever know who was on the other side of their contracts. The market is impersonal in this respect.

The Speculator

Now, we are in a position to take a closer look at one of the individuals who might take the role of B or C in Figures 1 and 2. This type of individual might well be a speculator. A speculator is someone who neither owns, nor desires to own, the commodity being traded. He assumes contractual ownership for a brief period of time solely in hopes of a favorable price fluctuation which would earn him a profit. By doing this, he provides the high trading volume necessary for an orderly market. All producers and all users of the physical commodity are likely to want to do the same thing at about the same time. Trading solely with each other would be, therefore, a very difficult process. Speculators provide the liquidity necessary for the rapid purchase or sale of commodity contracts. Without them, it might take days or weeks to complete a trade which now takes only minutes.

Let's pause here to review the Commodity Exchange functions. We have seen that the Exchange provides a central trading location, which makes the individual search process easier; records all transactions and supervises trading procedures, making the settlement of disputes easier; and publishes price information, giving all traders equal access to price quotations. All of these functions have developed in response to the basic need of commodity producers and handlers to transfer the risk of price fluctuation in an easy and efficient manner. The commodity futures market did not develop as a device for speculators. It developed as a mechanism for the benefit of producers and users of commodities, with speculators playing a helpful role.

The Basis

We have briefly examined the origin of the futures market; now, we will take a look at the factors which keep this market orderly. Of course, the regulation and supervision of the Commodity Exchange plays a vital role. This role keeps the mechanics of the marketplace orderly. The other factor necessary for a workable market is an orderly link between cash market prices and futures market prices. We will now look closely at this link and see how it functions. Figure 3 represents a highly simplified pattern of commodity price movement. Assuming that everyone in the

Figure 3.

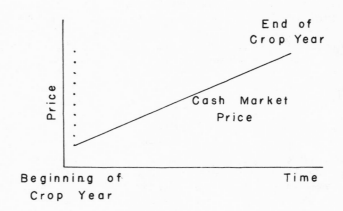

market has perfect knowledge, we would expect that, at the beginning of the crop year, when the crop is in abundant supply, price would be low. It would increase steadily as this supply was used up and storage charges were incurred, until it reached a peak at the end of the crop year when the supply was shortest.

What would a buyer be willing to pay for a commodity shipment at the beginning of the crop year if he were not going to use that shipment until the end of the crop year? Remember that everyone has perfect knowledge, so that he knows what price will prevail at the end of the crop year. He would be willing to pay a price which would allow him to at least break even on the storage of that commodity until he needed it; that is, a price that would be low enough to allow him to add on his carrying charges and still come out equal to or lower than the end of year price.

The seller, on the other hand, also knows the end of the crop year price. He will be willing to sell only at a price equal to or higher than that which he could earn by storing the commodity until the end of the crop year. In other words, he will sell at a price which allows him to add on his carrying charges and come out equal to or higher than the end of the year price.

The price which will be agreeable to both buyer and seller will, therefore, be the price which differs from the end of crop year price by exactly the amount of carrying charges. These carrying charges include storage costs, insurance costs, and the interest lost on the investment tied up in the crop. We may add these storage, insurance, and interest costs to the cash market price, as seen in Figure 4, to obtain the market's estimate of the future price for that crop.

Figure 4.

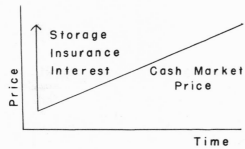

As time passes, these carrying charges will become less and less since the period of storage becomes shorter and shorter. In Figure 5, we see that the carrying charges gradually diminish over time. The top of each arrow represents an estimate of the future market price obtained by adding to the cash market price the carrying charges from the purchase date to the date of scheduled use. The date of use was defined here as the end of the crop year.

Figure 5.

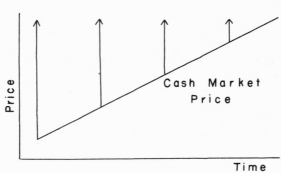

The futures market price then becomes the flat line that you see at the top of Figure 6. The futures market price may

Figure 6.

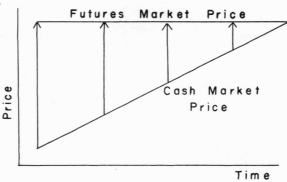

be thought of as the price a buyer would be willing to pay right now for a good that he would receive some time in the future. In an orderly market, he would be indifferent as to whether he would pay the higher futures market price and let someone else store the crop until he was ready for it, or whether he would pay the lower cash market price and undertake the storage himself. Remember that when an individual purchases a futures market contract, he does not actually take possession of the commodity until a specified future date. In an actual futures market, the delivery date is set by the standardized commodity contract.

The difference between the cash market price and the futures market price is called the basis. We know that it consists of storage, interest, and insurance charges. This is illustrated in Figure 7. The difference between the cash

Figure 7.

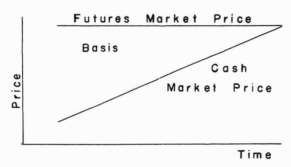

and futures market price at the beginning of the contract period will be large. As time goes on, the carrying charges to the contract expiration date will become smaller and, therefore, the difference between the cash market price and the futures market price narrows. At the stated contract expiration date the commodity is deliverable, so the cash and futures prices become identical. That is, the basis becomes zero.

We have assumed perfect price knowledge up to this point for purposes of simplification. When this assumption is dropped, expectations will play a role in price formulation. With uncertainty, both the cash market and the futures market price will fluctuate during the life of the contract. But, normally, the basis pattern will remain the same. The basis should reflect carrying charges at any point in time and will gradually diminish until it becomes zero at delivery. This pattern is illustrated for a fluctuating market in Figure 8.

Figure 8.

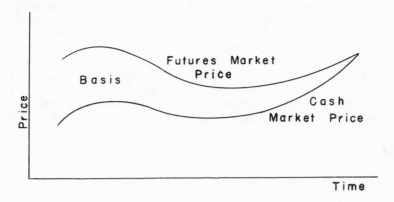

If conditions exist which will affect the future markets differently than they affect the current cash markets, then the basis may diverge from the traditional storage, interest, and insurance charges pattern. For example, a shortage of crop on hand, coupled with a large crop growing in the field, can actually force the cash price above the futures price. The short current supply drives the cash price up, while the expectation of a large harvest holds down the futures price. However, deviations from the traditional basis patterns are usually short-term in nature and cannot be completely arbitrary.

Producers often express the fear that speculators' expectations will control market prices. This is not the case as long as there is a workable delivery system. If speculators bid the future price of a commodity too high in relation to the actual market conditions, that is, if the basis were wider than carrying charges by a large amount, then producers of the commodity would simply sell the futures contract at the inflated price, hold the contract until expiration, and then actually deliver it. The speculator is not in a position to use the commodity and cannot afford to let this happen. If speculators drive the price of a commodity down too far in relation to the actual market conditions, that is, if the basis were too narrow, then users of the commodity would simply buy the futures contract at the depressed price and then demand that the speculators actually deliver the commodity to them. Thus, we see that the threat of delivery, or the threat of demanding delivery, guarantees an orderly relationship between cash market and futures market prices. Prices do not exist at the speculators' whim, but as a function of actual market conditions.

We can see now that the basis reflects storage costs, insurance costs, interest on the money tied up, and expectations. The basis, at any point in time, is equal to the difference between the futures market and the cash market prices.

Now that we understand the basic mechanics of the futures market and the factors which keep the market orderly, we are in a position to look at the operation of hedging.

Hedging ·

Hedging may be thought of as a device to provide protection against the risk of price fluctuations, much as a lawn hedge serves to protect property boundaries. It is not a mechanism by which the producer obtains something for nothing; it is a device which provides him with protection.

The formal definition of hedging is:

> "The process of offsetting an existing
> risk by taking an equal and opposite
> position on another risk likely to
> move in the same direction."

This is quite a mouthful. Let's take a look at it one piece at a time. The owner of a commodity has "an existing risk": the risk of price fluctuation. He can offset, or transfer, this risk by taking "an opposite position of equal size" in the futures market. If he is holding a crop, he sells a commodity futures contract. He has transferred the right of ownership and, therefore, the price risk, to someone else. Since this "other risk", the futures market is tied to the cash market by the basis, it is "likely to move in the same direction".

Another intuitive look at hedging may be helpful. Suppose that you have bet on the East in an upcoming East-West football game. That becomes your existing risk. Now, you decide that this bet is too risky for you because too much money is at stake. You can hedge your bet, or offset your risk, by placing another bet of equal size on the West with someone else. In this way, regardless of which team wins, you win your bet from one individual and pay off the bet to another. Of course, commodity hedging should not be thought of as gambling, since the producer does not create his risk

to start with. It is an unavoidable part of his business.
This betting analogy was constructed solely as an explanatory
aid.

Now, we can look at an actual hedge. Suppose that we
have an individual who is holding an agricultural commodity
which has an active futures market. He holds 5,000 units of
this commodity, and its current cash market price is $3 per
unit. He's not ready to sell the product right now, but he's
afraid that the market price will decline before he is ready
to move it on the cash market. He has an existing risk in
the cash market and can offset this by a futures contract
for 5,000 units at the current futures market price. We
know that because of the basis, this price should be higher
than the cash price. Let's assume that it is $3.15 per unit.

Cash Market	Futures Market
holds 5,000 units	sells 5,000 units
now worth $3.00/unit	at $3.15/unit

Four months later, he actually sells his 5,000 units
for the prevailing cash market price of $2.70 per unit. His
earlier fears were well founded: the market price has indeed
declined. Holding the physical commodity alone would have
netted him a 30¢ per unit loss. He also lifts his hedge
since he no longer has a cash market risk which needs pro-
tecting. He makes an offsetting trade by buying 5,000 units
in the futures market. We know that the futures price should
again be higher than the cash price and will assume it to be
$2.75 per unit. He has purchased a contract for $2.75 and
someone initially agreed to pay him $3.15. He has a net
profit of 40¢ on his futures transactions.

Cash Market		Futures Market
holds 5,000 units	⊤	sells 5,000 units
worth $3.00/unit		at $3.15/unit
	4 months	
sells 5,000 units		buys 5,000 units
at $2.70/unit	⊥	at $2.75/unit

30¢/unit loss	40¢/unit gain

net 10¢/unit "profit"

The producer's net "profit" from his hedge is 40¢-30¢, or 10¢ per unit. The word "profit" is placed in quotation marks since it must be used to offset the carrying costs incurred over the 4 months of product storage.

You will notice that the basis has changed over this period. Four months ago, it was $3.15 minus $3.00, or 15¢. Now it stands at $2.75 minus $2.70, or 5¢. The basis has narrowed by 10¢, which reflects the market's estimate of the carrying charges for this period. Someone must actually pay for product storage. The individual who pays is typically the one who has the title of ownership. In this example, the individual buying the futures contract has title of ownership over this period, and we would expect that he would pay an amount sufficient to cover the carrying charges. In fact, he has; this is the 10¢ which the producer received to cover his costs.

This can be a confusing point and we should consider the mechanism by which it takes place. The Clearing House does not bill the futures contract owner for the storage charges. He pays them because the price of the futures contract four months ago was higher than the cash market price by exactly the market's estimate of these carrying charges. In other words, four months ago the buyer agreed to pay the farmer the going cash market price plus an extra amount sufficient to cover storage until the contract expiration date. This is the basis concept discussed earlier.

We can now see what this hedge accomplished for the producer. It has:

(1) protected him against a price decline, and

(2) allowed him to earn carrying charges.

Our producer has "locked in" his $3.00 price at which he placed his hedge. He actually nets for his product:

        $2.70 sale price
    +   .40 futures market profit
    -    .10 carrying charges
        ─────
        $3.00/ unit.

It was noted earlier that a hedge does not provide the producer something for nothing. Failure to realize a loss when price declines also means failure to realize a windfall gain when price rises. Let's see how this same hedge would have looked in a rising market.

Cash Market	Futures Market
holds 5,000 units now worth $3.00/unit	sells 5,000 units at $3.15/unit

We have returned to the time of hedge placement with our producer still afraid of a price decline. Four months again elapses, but this time price increases. He sells his cash crop for $3.25 per unit and lifts his hedge at $3.30 per unit.

Cash Market	Futures Market
holds 5,000 units worth $3.00/unit	sells 5,000 units at $3.15/unit
4 months	
sells 5,000 units at $3.25/unit	buys 5,000 units at $3.30/unit
25¢/unit gain	15¢/unit loss

net 10¢/unit "profit"

His net "profit", which may be used to offset carrying charges, is once again 10¢. The basis at the time of hedge placement was $3.15 minus $3.00, or 15¢; the basis now is $3.30 minus $3.25, or 5¢. The basis has once again narrowed by 10¢. The basis pattern has remained the same even though the direction of price movement has not. Our producer did not receive a windfall gain from the price increase, but he still "locked in" his $3.00 cash price. His net is now:

$3.25   sale price
− .15   futures market loss
− .10   carrying charges
———
$3.00/ unit.

Now the list of hedging accomplishments may be revised to:

    (1)   protect against price <u>changes</u>, and

    (2)   earn carrying charges.

Producer Speculation

Let's look once more at the type of individual who might buy the promise to deliver sold in the previous hedging example. Typically, we think of this person as a speculator. He might be a doctor, housewife, lawyer, or anyone outside the cash commodity market. But a speculator can be a producer, processor, or user of the commodity being traded. Simple participation in the commodity production and marketing channel does not guarantee that every futures market trade will be a hedge. Any one of these individuals can easily become a speculator. Remember that to have a hedge, a trader must take an equal offsetting position in the futures market. Let's consider a producer and see how he might use the futures market as a speculative tool.

Suppose a producer has just harvested his commodity, but is unable to find storage space. He is forced to sell his crop immediately for lack of storage. However, he feels that the market price is going up and he would like to profit from the expected rise. He was willing to speculate on the cash market by holding his crop for a later sale, but he could not. He can assume a similar speculation by purchasing a futures contract. He has no offsetting position since he no longer owns any cash commodity. Now he is just like any other speculator. He profits from a price rise and loses from a price decline.

Market Information

We have seen that hedgers may offset a price risk which exists in the cash market and that speculators may assume this risk in pursuit of a profit. Now we will consider a new, and often neglected, function of the commodity futures market: anyone may use the market reporting services which accompany futures trading to obtain current commodity information.

Commodity futures traders need reliable, current information and the media responds to this need. The market reports which are generated serve not only those trading in the futures market, but those trading in the cash market as well. A futures market does not necessarily generate new

information, but it almost certainly improves the timely dis-
tribution of information. This benefits everyone concerned
with the production and marketing of the traded commodities.

Typical sources of information include U.S. Government
reports, U.S.D.A. reports, and State weather reports. The
Commodity Exchange, itself, furnishes price quotations and
volume data. There are also many publications by trade
associations, cooperatives, and other commodity handlers.
Several brokerage houses and universities publish market
newsletters which provide up-to-date situation summaries,
as well as indications of likely future price trends. News-
papers and industry periodicals are also important sources.
Finally, anyone desiring the most current information has it
at hand as near as his telephone. A simple call to a local
broker's office can provide all the current information
which is available.

2

A FEW ESSENTIAL DETAILS

Although the previous chapter provides a conceptual base for understanding the futures market, it does not give a complete picture of the mechanics of trading. This chapter will discuss three aspects of this market which often cause confusion for the new trader: short selling, the margin account, and the reading of published price information.

Short Selling

Most new traders find no difficulty in understanding how a hedger can sell futures contracts. After all, he could actually deliver the commodity if he had to. But, what about the speculator? How can he sell a futures contract? Doesn't he have to buy a contract before he can sell it? No, he does not. A speculator may initiate a trade by selling in the futures market, even though he does not have any commodity to back up his commitment. He is merely promising that he will close out his position by making an offsetting trade before the contract expiration date. When he purchases contracts to offset his original sale, he is removed from the active record books and need not take part in the delivery process.

This process of selling something which we don't have has many parallels in our daily life. For example, when you subscribe to a magazine, the publisher does not have future issues in his inventory. He is merely promising to live up to his obligation at the appropriate time in the future. The speculator who sells a futures contract is making the same sort of promise. He is merely promising to make an offsetting trade at the appropriate time to avoid having to deliver. If he is able to buy for less than the original selling price, he makes a profit.

The speculator does run a small extra risk in doing this. If he should not be able to make this offsetting trade for one reason or another, he might be forced to deliver. In that case, he would buy the physical commodity in the cash market and deliver it. In a high volume market, this rarely, if ever, would occur.

Consider another parallel, the parallel between a hedge account and a speculative account. Most hedgers will offset an original sale in the futures market with an equivalent volume purchase in the futures market before delivery time. They will then market their cash crop locally. The fact that they actually had the crop in their inventory was relevant only to their own profit-and-loss statement. As far as the futures market was concerned, the fact that they owned the cash commodity was irrelevant. A speculative account would have looked just the same: a sale followed by an offsetting purchase. The difference would become apparent only at delivery time and, remember, that over 99 percent of all contracts avoid the delivery mechanism entirely.

There is nothing mysterious about speculators selling in the futures market. It just takes a little time before producers feel comfortable with the notion.

The Margin Account

All trading in the commodity market is done on margin. The trader does not put up the full value of the contract when he buys or sells it. He puts up only a fraction of the total value, called his margin. The margin is a reserve against default and serves the same purpose as earnest money in a real estate deal. If the customer earns a profit at the completion of his trade, his full margin, plus his profit, minus a small broker's commission, is returned to him. If he has accumulated a loss, the broker's commission, plus his loss, are deducted from the initial margin and the balance is returned. The initial margin typically amounts to 10 percent or less of the total contract value. However, the amount varies from commodity to commodity, depending on the price volatility and risk involved. The minimum margin requirement is set at a stated dollar amount by the Commodity Exchange and remains fixed until the Exchange explicitly changes it.

There are two types of margins: the initial margin, already discussed, and a maintenance margin. Since the margin account functions as a reserve against loss, the account cannot be allowed to decline to zero before action is taken. If a loss larger than the initial account is allowed to accumulate, the customer could default and leave an uncollectible debt. The Exchange prevents this from happening by setting a maintenance margin requirement. The maintenance margin is a stated dollar amount which must remain in the account after all losses are deducted from the initial margin. Should the account reach the maintenance level, the broker is required to contact the customer and ask him to bring his account back to its initial level. This is known as a margin call. If he refuses, cannot be located, or requests that his account be closed, the broker makes an offsetting trade for him and refunds the balance of his account. The maintenance level gives the broker time to locate his customer and close the account, if necessary, before the reserve drops to zero.[2/]

This is a very efficient system. There is no recorded loss due to default on any account traded on a regulated commodity futures market in the United States. The only problem which could occur under this system is the bankruptcy of a brokerage house which had misused margin accounts. On the rare occasions on which this has occurred, the remaining member houses have made good any customer losses resulting from the bankruptcy.

Margin accounts are closely supervised by the Commodity Exchange. Margin money collected by the brokers must be placed in a segregated account and cannot be used for other purposes by the brokerage house. These accounts are audited regularly by the Exchange.

Two special features of the margin account should be understood by producers. First, large accounts need not put up cash for margin. Most houses will accept treasury bills instead. In this way, the trader can continue to draw interest on his money tied up in the margin account. Second, if the trade accumulates a paper profit, the customer can draw out his profit if it is in excess of his margin require-ments. In this way, he can enjoy some of the fruits of a profitable trade without having to close out his position.

Reading Published Price Reports

The commodity market has its own system of notation and the trader is expected to be familiar with it. Two typical commodity listings are presented in Table 1.

Consider the wheat first. Four contract delivery months are now trading: July, September, December, and March of 1973. These prices were recorded in May of 1972. The trading units for wheat are cents per bushel, so the July

---

[2/] Margin requirements change frequently and a broker should be consulted for current figures. However, it is helpful to have some idea of the relative magnitude. A traditional requirement for one 5,000 bushel contract of wheat has been a $600 initial margin and a $400 maintenance level.

TABLE 1. A Typical Price Report.

	Open	High	Low	Close	Change	Season's High	Season's Low
CHICAGO—WHEAT							
July.......	$146^5/_8$	$147^5/_8$	$145^3/_4$	$147^3/_8-^1/_2$	$-^1/_8$ to unch	$153^1/_4$	$135^5/_8$
Sept.......	$148^3/_8$	$149^1/_8$	$147^1/_4$	$148^3/_4$	$-^1/_8$	155	$138^7/_8$
Dec........	$152^1/_2$	$153^5/_8$	$151^1/_4$	$153-153^1/_4$	$-^1/_2$ to $^1/_4$	$159^3/_4$	$145^1/_4$
Mar'73.....	$154^3/_8$	$155^1/_4$	$153^1/_2$	$154^1/_2$	$-^5/_8$	161	$150^1/_8$
CATTLE (CHICAGO MERCANTILE EXCHANGE)							
June.......	37.00	37.10	36.92	37.05-.07	+.08to.10	37.10	30.80
Aug........	35.67	35.75	35.60	35.72-.75	+.07to.10	35.80	30.70
Oct........	34.47	34.50	34.40	34.50	+.05	34.67	30.75
Dec........	34.50	34.57	34.45	34.55-.57	+.10to.12	34.80	31.00
Feb'73.....	34.85	34.95	34.77	34.90-.95	+.05to.10	34.45	32.00
Apr........	34.70	34.70	34.52	34.65	.....	34.75	32.35

Sales estimated at: 2,716 contracts.

28

contract opened the day's trading at $1.46^5/$_8$ per bushel.
This means that the first trade of the day was made at this
price. The highest price of the day for this contract
reached $1.47^5/$_8$; the lowest price of the day reached
$1.45^3/$_4$; and, at the closing bell, the contract stood at
$1.47^3/$_8$ bid and $1.47^1/$_2$ asked. This means that no trades
were being made at the closing, but buyers were willing to
pay $1.47^3/$_8$ per bushel, and sellers were asking $1.47^1/$_2$.
The change column indicates the change from the previous
trading day's close to the current closing price. There are
two numbers in the change column for this contract because of
the two numbers representing today's closing price. The bid
is down ^{1}/$_8$, while the asked is the same as the closing price
for the previous trading day. The last two columns indicate
that the highest price received for a July contract, since it
started trading, was $1.53^1/$_4$, and the lowest price was
$1.35^5/$_8$. There is no uniform starting date for these con-
tracts and a broker would have to be consulted to find the
exact starting date, if this were desired.

One contract of Chicago wheat is 5,000 bushels. This
means that one July contract was worth a total of $7368.75
(5000 x 1.47^3/$_8$), using the closing bid.

Consider now the cattle contract. Six contract delivery
months are now active, from June of 1972 to April of 1973.
The trading units for cattle are dollars per hundredweight,
so the June contract opened the day's trading at $37.00 per
hundredweight. All other prices follow the scheme discussed
for wheat. Each contract delivery month is traded and quoted
separately.

One contract of live cattle is 40,000 pounds. This
means that one June contract was worth a total of $14,820
(400 cwt. x 37.05), using the closing bid.

The number of contracts traded is not always reported.
It is listed for the cattle contract as 2,716. This means
that 2,716 contracts were purchased and 2,716 were sold on
that trading day. Since the contracts are in standard volume
units, the number purchased and the number sold are always
equal.

The wheat contracts show a standard basis pattern:
price increases as the delivery months become more distant.
This follows from increasingly larger carrying charges, month-
by-month. However, the cattle contracts diminish in price
over time. This pattern will be discussed under the heading

Nonstorable Commodities at the end of this chapter.

It should be clear that the trader needs to know the price units and standard contract volume in order to interpret published price reports. Table 2 lists this information for most commodities having an active futures market.

TABLE 2. Contract Units and Sizes.

Commodity	Pricing Units	Contract Size
Broilers (Iced).......	Dollars/cwt.	28,000 lbs.
Cattle (Feeder).......	Dollars/cwt.	42,000 lbs.
Cattle (Live).........	Dollars/cwt.	40,000 lbs.
Cocoa.................	Cents/lb.	30,000 lbs.
Corn.................	Dollars/bu.	5,000 bu.
Cotton...............	Cents/lb.	50,000 lbs.
Eggs.................	Cents/doz.	22,500 doz.
Hogs (Live)..........	Dollars/cwt.	30,000 lbs.
Oats.................	Dollars/bu.	5,000 bu.
Plywood (Chicago).....	Dollars/1,000 sq.ft.	69,120 sq.ft.
Pork Bellies..........	Cents/lb.	36,000 lbs.
Potatoes.............	Dollars/cwt.	50,000 lbs.
Soybeans.............	Dollars/bu.	5,000 bu.
Soybean Meal.........	Dollars/ton	100 tons
Soybean Oil..........	Cents/lb.	60,000 lbs.
Sugar (World)........	Cents/lb.	112,000 lbs.
Wheat................	Cents/bu.	5,000 bu.

Table 3 gives the standard trading months for these same contracts. The data in Table 2 and in Table 3 are subject to change from time to time. A commodity broker can supply the most recent information.

TABLE 3. Contract Delivery Months.

Commodity	Active Delivery Months
Broilers (Iced).....	Jan, Mar, May, Jul, Sep, Nov
Cattle (Feeder).....	Jan, May, Aug, Sep, Oct, Nov, Dec
Cattle (Live).......	Feb, Apr, Jun, Aug, Oct, Dec
Cocoa..............	Mar, May, Jul, Sep, Dec
Corn...............	Mar, May, Jul, Sep, Dec
Cotton.............	Mar, May, Jul, Oct, Dec
Eggs...............	Jan, Sep, Oct, Nov, Dec
Hogs (Live)........	Jul, Aug, Sep, Oct, Nov, Dec
Oats...............	Mar, May, Jul, Sep, Dec
Plywood (Chicago)...	Jan, Mar, May, Jul, Sep, Dec
Pork Bellies.......	Feb, Mar, May, Jul, Aug
Potatoes...........	Mar, Apr, May, Nov
Soybeans...........	Jan, Mar, May, Jul, Aug, Sep, Nov
Soybean Meal & Oil..	Jan, Mar, May, Jul, Aug, Sep, Oct, Dec
Sugar (World).......	Jan, Mar, May, Jul, Sep, Nov
Wheat..............	Mar, May, Jul, Sep, Dec

One more piece of information will prove valuable in
interpreting price reports. Each commodity has a maximum
allowable change from the previous day's closing price. Each
contract states this limit which varies from commodity to
commodity. The limit is designed to prevent panic buying and
selling from running away with a market. Once the limit is
reached, no contracts may be traded above that price if the
market has advanced to the upper limit, or below that price
if the market has declined to the lower limit. For example,
the limit in wheat is ±10 cents. If today's closing price is
$1.45, then contracts on tomorrow's market may only trade
within the range $1.35 to $1.55.

Trading is only suspended for prices outside the limit
once it is reached. If later trades are made at or inside
the stated limit, they are allowed. Table 4 presents the
current limits.

TABLE 4.   Contract Trading Limits.

Commodity	Allowable Fluctuation Above Or Below Previous Closing Price
Broilers (Iced)....................	2¢
Cattle (Feeder)....................	1¢
Cattle (Live).....................	1¢
Cocoa............................	1¢ a/
Corn.............................	8¢
Cotton...........................	2¢ a/
Eggs.............................	2¢
Hogs (Live).......................	$1^1/_2$¢
Oats.............................	8¢
Plywood (Chicago).................	$7.00 a/
Pork Bellies......................	$1^1/_2$¢
Potatoes..........................	35¢ b/
Soybeans..........................	10¢
Soybean Meal......................	$5.00 a/
Soybean Oil.......................	$33.00 a/
Sugar (World).....................	1/2¢
Wheat.............................	10¢

a/No limit in delivery month.

b/50¢ on last two trading days.

Nonstorable Commodities

Many commodities now traded on the futures market are
not storable in the sense that a commodity like grain is
storable. Live cattle, iced broilers, and pork bellies are
examples. These commodities are either too perishable to
store, or cannot be delivered after long storage, as specified in the commodity contract.

There are no carrying charges built into the basis for
these commodities as we have previously defined carrying
charges in terms of storable commodities. Instead, a historical basis pattern evolves which may be unique for each commodity of this type. In fact, the normal condition for a
nonstorable commodity may be cash over futures. Because cash
market delivery is generally more convenient and more reliable
than futures market delivery, the cash market may command a
slight premium. Basis patterns in nonstorable commodities
depend primarily on expectations and on historical relation-

ships. Cattle prices in Table 1 exhibit the influence of
expectations. The price generally declines as the delivery
months become more distant. This means that the market is
anticipating lower beef prices at the farm level in the year
ahead.

3

THE TRADING PROCESS

The actual mechanics of buying or selling a commodity futures contract are extremely simple once an account has been established. In fact, the process is so easy that the customer may be lulled into a false sense of security. It is absolutely essential that the trader be familiar with the language of the marketplace so that he can understand exactly what his obligations and liabilities are. This chapter will provide that information.

Financial Leverage

The first step in the trading process is a visit to a local commodity broker. After a brief discussion of trading objectives, the customer will be asked to sign an agreement card specifying the nature of financial liabilities. The broker will then open an account, sometimes accompanied by an investigation of the customer's net worth, and establish the margin requirements.

As mentioned in the previous chapter, the margin account represents "good faith" money and performs the same function that earnest money performs in a real estate deal. It is there to protect the financial commitment, should the customer default. An example will illustrate the operation of the margin account.

Suppose that a customer purchases one contract (5,000) bushels of December grain on August 15th at $1.20 per bushel. December grain simply means that the contract is scheduled for December delivery. The broker requires an initial margin of $600 and sets a maintenance margin of $400. At the time of purchase, the buyer deposits the required $600. On August 20th, the futures price has fallen to $1.19 per bushel for a loss of $50. The broker takes note of the deteriorating position, but since $550 of the margin remains after the loss is covered, he takes no action. On August 30th, the price falls to $1.15 for a total loss of $250 on the contract. The margin remaining after the loss is deducted now stands at $350. This is less than the maintenance requirement, so the broker asks his client to bring his margin account back to its initial value of $600. If he refuses, defaults, or re-quests a sale, the broker will sell one contract to offset his initial purchase. The loss and the broker's commission will be deducted from the $600 which the broker is holding, and the balance will be remitted to the customer.

It is important for the trader to realize that he may be required to supplement his margin account should the market move against him. Some funds must be held in reserve to meet this contingency.

Trading on margin creates financial leverage. This term is used often in the financial press, and we should take a little time to understand it. Leverage in financial terms is the control of a large sum of money with only a small investment or down payment. To see what this means, let's consider the previous example. Our speculator has purchased approximately $6,000 worth of grain but has provided a contingency fund of only $600 of his own money. Suppose the price of grain increases only 10 percent. The contract value is now $6,600 for a profit of $600, less a small commission charge. The grain price has risen only 10 percent, but our trader has a return on his investment of 100 percent. Any market movement is magnified in the trader's profit and loss statement. This helps to explain why a commodity trader needs to be very alert to price movements. It takes only relatively minor market fluctuations to completely wipe out his initial margin fund or to yield him a very large return on his investment. This also helps to explain why speculators find this market so attractive. The leverage in this market is much greater than it is in many other financial markets.

There is another important use of the margin requirements which has not been discussed. One very common fault of commodity speculators is to commit too large a portion of their trading capital on a single transaction. The margin requirements may be used to prevent overcommitment by establishing the number of contracts which should be traded. This calculation is especially important for a new commodity speculator who is used to trading 100 share lots on the stock exchange. The size of even one contract in commodities can be very substantial.

Let's assume that a trader has a speculative fund of $6,000 which he has set aside for trading. He decides that it would be safe to expose 15 percent of this on any one trade. This means that he can commit $900 (6,000 x .15). He decides to buy grain because he feels that the price will rise, but he also realizes that a slight drop would trigger a margin call and force him out of the market before his anticipated price rise finally starts. He decides that he will meet one margin call before undergoing a major re-evaluation of his position. Using the margin figures established in the previous example, a $200 loss would trigger such a margin call. This means that he will risk $200 on the first margin call, which he will meet, plus a maximum loss of another $200, which would trigger a second margin call and close out his position. This total risk exposure of $400 per contract means that he may purchase two contracts and still be within his safety limit. Two contracts would expose $800 to loss, which is within the $900 limit per trade which he set for himself. Of course, he must still put up an initial $1200 ($600 per contract) to make the purchase. But his decision to meet only one margin call means that he would not stand to lose all of this. If the worst happened, he would still reclaim the remaining $400 of his margin account after his $800 loss was deducted.

It is not unusual for traders to purchase only one or two contracts in the futures market. A simple calculation of the type just illustrated should help the trader to develop a realistic assessment of the trading volume which he can safely handle.

The calculation just illustrated would be most helpful to a speculator. The decision process is somewhat different for a hedger. He is not worried how much risk to assume, but how to offset his existing cash market risk. He should purchase the number of contracts which most closely approximates the volume of cash commodity held. Ordinarily, he will trade in the contract month which is the first to expire after the anticipated time of his cash market liquidation. Special situations may alter this rule of thumb and a broker should be consulted before selecting the proper delivery month for the hedge contract.

Types of Orders

Once the appropriate number of contracts and the trading month have been established, the type of order to be placed must be selected. The common order designations follow.

Market Order. A market order directs the floor broker to fill the order at the best market price as soon as it reaches the floor of the exchange. This is the basic order of the marketplace. If no special instructions are given by the customer, the broker assumes that he is placing a market order.

Limit Order. This term refers to a price limitation imposed by the customer. It is to be executed only as a stated price, or at one more favorable to the customer. If the market price is less favorable than the limit price, the order is not executed. For example, if a limit order to buy at $3.00 were placed, the purchase could be executed at less than $3.00, but not at more than this limit.

Off At A Specified Time Order. This is an order which expires at a specific time if unfilled. For example: buy until 11:00 a.m.

Stop Order. This order directs the floor broker to execute a market order if the prices reach a specified limit set by the customer. These may be used either to enter or to exit the market. Historically, they have been used to prevent excessive losses and, hence, their common name, Stop Loss Orders. The Stop Order merely remains in the broker's file until its specified price is reached. It is then activated and executed as a market order. If the market never reaches the specified price, the order is never activated. No commission is paid unless the Stop Order is filled.

Market If Touched Order. A Market If Touched Order (MIT) is typically a device used to enter the market at a predetermined level. Like a Stop Order, it directs the floor broker to execute the order once the market price reaches a specified level. Unlike a pure Stop Order, it does not become a Market Order, but instead may be filled only at the specified price or at one more favorable to the customer. This type of order may also be called a Board Order.

There are two more order designations which are important for the trader to understand. Either of these designations may be added to any of the other order types.

Day Order. A Day Order expires with the end of the day's trading. If it has not been filled, it does not carry into the next trading day. Most orders are assumed to be Day Orders, unless otherwise specified when the order is placed.

Open Order. The designation Open Order attached to an order means that it is to remain active until it is filled, or until the original customer explicitly issues a cancellation. It does carry from trading session to trading session. This is sometimes known as a Good Until Cancelled (GTC) Order.

A market order may be placed as a day order, or as an open order. In most cases, this is an irrelevant designation because the order is executed immediately after it reaches the floor. However, open orders might be used for orders placed very late in the day in a slow trading market, or for orders placed on days when a limit move is likely.

The broker can help the customer select the right type of order to meet his objectives. But it is up to the customer to understand the obligations implied by each type. There is no room for a careless phrase when placing an order.

Stocks Versus Commodities

Now that you understand the basic mechanics of futures trading, it is time to take a broader look at the market. It will be useful to contrast commodity trading with stock market investing. Many of you are familiar with stock trading and there are some trading techniques useful in that market which must not be carried over into commodity futures trading.

One of the more obvious differences between the two markets is the attitude toward short selling. Most novices enter the commodity futures market on the long side. At least part of the reason for this is a carry-over from the logic of the stock market. Short sellers profit from a price decline, and a decline in the price of stock typically means that the company is in trouble. Charges of "feeding on the misery of others" were commonly endured by the shorts during the 1929 market crash. The stigma against the short selling of stocks is strong enough to support several sanctions against the practice. For example: Short sales do not enjoy capital gains status; the short seller must pay any dividends declared by the company; sales may be made only on a price uptick; and borrowed shares must be placed on deposit with a broker to cover any short sales.

No such sanctions exist in the commodity market.[3] In fact, a price decline in the commodity market often reflects good weather and high yields. No one would fault a short for profiting from that state of affairs. There is another condition which favors short sellers in the commodity market. Delivery is at the option of the seller. At any time during

------

[3] There is an exception to this: Short sales still do not enjoy capital gains status. This rule does not usually apply since most commodity positions are held for less than six months.

the contract delivery month, the short may give notice of his intention to deliver. This notice is passed on to the oldest open long in that commodity. The oldest open long is the buyer who has held an open contract for the longest period of time. Of course, delivery can only be made to buyers holding open contracts for the same commodity and the same delivery month as the seller who is delivering. Once he receives a notice, the long generally has a chance to avoid the actual delivery if he acts quickly enough. The actual process varies from one commodity to another. Typically, the long can close out his position within a time limit of a few hours and pay a small penalty fee. Because of this delivery mechanism, a short trader can carry his contract up to the stated expiration date (usually the 20th of the month). However, a long has no control over the timing of delivery and will often prefer to close out his position before the first notice day of the delivery month.

Any trader who uses only one side of the market severely limits his profit opportunities. A new trader must learn to be equally comfortable with short sales as with long sales.

Another misunderstanding often arises from the stock market concept of margin trading. Margin trading in stocks means that the buyer supplies only a portion of the stock value in cash and borrows the rest from his broker. An interest charge on the loan is levied by the broker. People familiar with this system often feel that margin money is not required on short sales of commodity futures. They reason that since they haven't really purchased anything, no down payment is required. Once you see that the commodity market margin is a reserve against loss, it is easy to see that it is required on a short, as well as a long, sale. Two more differences between the markets exist. These are of a more fundamental nature than the two just discussed.

When you invest in stocks you can hold them for the "long pull", a period of several years. If a particular stock declines in value, it is often possible to keep this stock in your portfolio for a year or two until it appreciates. In this fashion, a bad short-term decision may be turned into a good long-term one. This phenomenon has prompted some market analysts to say that the only long-term investors are unsuccessful short-term speculators. This option is not open to the commodity trader since each contract ceases to exist at the stated expiration date. This means that the commodity trader cannot bury his mistakes and wait for a joyful resurrection some years later. A paper loss cannot be put away to be forgotten.

You are now in a position to realize why the phrase commodity market trader is used in place of commodity market investor. This is done to indicate that one cannot invest in commodity futures contracts in the usual long-term sense. If the commodity trader cannot ignore his losses, what can he do? The answer is simple to say, but hard to do. He must continually monitor his transactions. When he is wrong, he must admit his mistake and get out fast. Small losses must be taken to prevent any further deterioration of his position. In the stock market, the decisions of which stock to buy and when to buy it are the most important part of the investment process. In the commodity market, these decisions are only one-half the job. The other half is constant monitoring of the market and constant reappraisal of the original buy-sell decision.

Fortunately, the job of watching the market is a little easier in the case of commodities. This brings us to the last major difference between the futures market and the stock market. There are only about two dozen actively traded commodity contracts versus over 1200 stocks listed on the New York Stock Exchange alone. In stocks, it is possible to know that the market trend is strongly up and still not be able to pick an individual winner. In the futures market, each commodity forms a market of its own. The job of analysis is a little easier when the number of markets which must be watched is reasonably small.

4
TRADERS AND THEIR OBJECTIVES

The Commodity Futures Market serves many different types of traders with many different objectives. We will explore the more important characteristics and methods of the two basic trading groups, hedgers and speculators. This material is designed for producers of agricultural commodities whose trading would normally be classified as hedging. Nevertheless, an extensive discussion of speculators and their techniques is essential. First of all, speculators form an important part of the marketplace, and we should understand their motives. Second, and most important, all successful hedgers have the urge at some point in their investment careers to speculate independently from their farm business. One objective of this book is to develop an understanding of the futures market. Another is to help producers appreciate the great risks associated with a purely speculative plan of action.

Hedgers

A hedger[4] is an individual who uses the futures market in conjunction with cash market transactions involving the same commodity. He holds an inventory of the cash crop either in storage or growing, or plans to acquire such an inventory in the near future. In other words, he is in a business which requires a cash crop inventory as part of the day-to-day operations. His business needs are his first consideration and any futures market transactions are undertaken to help meet these needs. For example, the hedger may use the futures market to shift the risk of inventory price fluctuations to someone else. He is then able to concentrate on normal production operations without the worry of adverse price movements.

Make no mistake about it, profit is the motive behind hedging transactions. But the profit comes from the business operations; the futures market merely allows the producer the flexibility to take advantage of that profit. Hedging will not save an unprofitable business. It can, however, improve an already profitable one. This point is difficult to grasp at first. But once you understand this, it becomes clear that

---

[4] Hedging is defined on page 17.

there are no magical profits to be had from the futures market. Successful futures trading is undertaken as an integral part of the production process. It should not be added on merely as an afterthought.

Think of a hedge as a substitute for a cash market transaction. Whenever a crop is harvested, or an inventory purchased, the manager's prime concern is a cash market sale. However, a profitable cash sale may not be available at that time. The futures market may then be used as a substitute for the cash sale to be made at a later date. A simple example will illustrate this principle.

An egg producer is just starting a new operation and plans to have 22,500 dozen eggs produced and ready for market one month from now. He calculates that his total cost will be 30 cents per dozen. Of course, the eggs are not ready for sale now and cannot be disposed of on the cash market for one month. Our producer sees that the futures market price for eggs to be delivered next month is 34 cents per dozen and falling. Fearing a cash price below his cost at market time, he hedges his eggs. The transaction looks like this:

CASH MARKET	FUTURES MARKET
plans to have 22,500 dozen at 30¢/dozen cost	sell 22,500 dozen at 34¢/dozen

Let's see if this transaction meets our definition of a hedge. The producer had an existing risk in the cash market, the first condition of our definition. He has taken an opposite position on another risk by selling an equal amount in the futures market, the second condition of our definition. And, since the cash and futures prices are influenced by the same conditions, they are likely to move in the same direction. This is a valid hedge. Our producer can now concentrate on his productive process free from the worry of a price deterioration. How did he know whether to buy or sell the futures contracts? This question can always be resolved if the producer asks himself the question: What am I afraid of in the cash market? In this case, he is afraid of a price decline and protects himself with a sale in the futures market. If he were confident of a price rise, he would have no reason to seek protection and would not hedge his production.

Suppose that our producer's fears were well-grounded, and that price does decline to 25¢/dozen at market time. He sells his eggs and lifts his hedge with the following results:

CASH MARKET	FUTURES MARKET
plans to have 22,500 dozen at 30¢/dozen cost	sells 22,500 dozen at 34¢/dozen
sells 22,500 dozen at 25¢/dozen	buys 22,500 dozen at 25¢/dozen
5¢/dozen loss	9¢/dozen gain

overall profit
4¢/dozen

The 4¢ per dozen profit came from producing eggs at a cost of 4¢ less than the going price a month ago. The futures transaction "locked in" the price at that time; it did not create the profit. Had our producer's cost been higher than the going market price, he would have "locked in" a loss with his hedge. A hedge cannot turn a loss in the cash market into a profit. It can, however, allow a producer to set a price for his product before it is ready for sale on the cash market. Hedging provides valuable marketing flexibility.

Let's now consider our hedger's results in a rising market. Suppose the price had not fallen, but, instead, had risen to 38¢ per dozen by market time. The completed hedge now produces the following results:

CASH MARKET	FUTURES MARKET
plans to have 22,500 dozen at 30¢/dozen cost	sells 22,500 dozen at 34¢/dozen
sells 22,500 dozen at 38¢/dozen	buys 22,500 dozen at 38¢/dozen
8¢/dozen gain	4¢/dozen loss

overall profit
4¢/dozen

Our hedger has once again earned his 4¢ profit margin, but he obtained this protection at a cost. Freedom from worry about price fluctuation means failure to reap a windfall gain from a price rise, as well as protection from loss in a falling market. In this case, his overall profit would have been 8¢ per dozen without the hedge. You can see that price forecasting plays a role, even in hedging. When you hedge, you are saying that you are willing to sell your cash crop at that price. The same management decision process is involved in hedging as in actually selling the crop on the spot market. However, a hedge does provide more flexibility in reversing this decision at a later date. It is much easier to reverse a hedge than to reverse a forward pricing arrangement made in the cash market.

Several other hedging examples will be discussed in greater detail in the next chapter. Let us now turn to the second major group of traders.

Speculators

Speculators are the most misunderstood group in the commodities market. The typical layman considers the speculator to be a worthless gambler and price manipulator. This is certainly not the case. A gambler creates his own risks through his games and society is none the better for the process. A speculator assumes an existing risk, not of his own making, and society benefits. An inescapable risk is shifted to the person best able to bear it. An analogy would be the assumption of the risk of fire by insurance companies. These companies are speculating on the risk of fire, but their operation is highly beneficial to the insured parties. In the same sense, speculators function in commodity futures market to insure hedgers against the risk of price fluctuations. Of course, they do this in hopes of profit, but their actions help all members of the trade. In fact, there could be no commodity futures market without speculators. Their trading volume provides the market liquidity which allows hedging to take place.

The speculator also performs another valuable function, price validation. Since a speculator neither owns nor desires to own the commodity being traded, his sole means of acquiring profit is through better forecasting and interpretation of impending events than the average trader. This sensitivity to the changing conditions of demand and supply helps to assure that the prices quoted are as meaningful and accurate as possible. In retrospect, we may judge that a given market price was not justified. But, at the time it was quoted, we may be assured that it accurately reflected the best judgment of the marketplace. A price quoted in the futures market should not be thought of as an actual forecast of prices in the delivery period since many unforeseen events may occur before actual delivery. Instead, a futures price should be thought of as the price someone is willing to pay right now, based on an analysis of current facts, for goods to be delivered at the specified later date. This is a subtle point, but it establishes the need to re-evaluate your position when one of these major unforeseen events occur.

Speculators do not act in unison to the detriment of those actually holding the commodity. It is a myth that speculators act as a group to drive prices to excessive highs or lows merely for their own profit. Each speculator is acting independently on his own assessment of the market. Any deviation from the dictates of supply and demand by one group of speculators would be rapidly offset by other speculators who knew the true value of the commodity. Only in very small, inactive markets would any group of speculators be able to control price. This very lack of volume would be enough to discourage hedgers and keep them out of harm's way.

We have been talking about speculators in the collective sense. Let us now look at the different types of speculators operating in the market.

Scalpers. Scalpers are members of the exchange and trade in the commodity pit for their own accounts. They quickly assume and liquidate large volumes for even the smallest margins. Their profit is dependent upon a rapid turnover rate, and they are, therefore, very valuable in providing market liquidity.

Day Traders. Day traders also trade in the pit for their own account. They end each day with an even balance of contracts and do not carry any positions into the next day's trading session. The day trader holds a position longer than a scalper, hoping to detect trends which will provide larger profit margins.

Position Traders. This is the name given to the group most people have in mind when they think of speculators. These are the non-professional traders, the doctors, housewives, etc., who place their orders through brokers. They typically take a position in the market and hold it for several days or months.

Spreaders. Spreaders are the most sophisticated group of speculators. The spreader maintains a history of normal price relationships between contract delivery months, between major market centers, and between related commodities. When prices deviate from the spreaders notion of normal patterns, he buys in the low market and sells in the high one. He then makes a small profit if the prices return to their historical relationship. Spreaders help to maintain cash market prices and futures market prices in their proper relationship. An example of one type of spread will illustrate the process.

Suppose a spreader observes an early September price of 122 for December grain and 129 for March grain. His records indicate a normal difference of 6 cents between the two months which reflects actual carrying charges. This means that the existing spread is too wide. Anticipating a return to the normal relationship, our trader sells the high-priced month and buys the low. Five days later prices have declined, but the December-March prices have resumed their historical pattern.

DECEMBER CONTRACT	MARCH CONTRACT
Buy at 122	Sell at 129
Sell at 120	Buy at 126
2¢ per bu. loss	3¢ per bu. gain

The spreader made a net gain of 1 cent per bushel on the transaction. Although his profit opportunity was very small, so was his risk. Since the spread is a low risk operation, the margin requirements are also reduced.

Straddlers. A spread which does not involve two grains is called a straddle.

Although producers tend to think of speculators as very wise and successful traders, the record does not bear this out. In fact, the vast majority of trades made by speculators lose money. Then why do they continue to trade? Remember that the leverage is considerable in commodity futures trading. Speculators appear to be willing to exchange a series of losses for the possibility of being on the correct side of a big move and reaping enormous profits.

The objective of the speculator is to make money in the futures market. The hedger, on the other hand, has a different set of goals in mind. He will want to:

(1)   Improve his market timing, or

(2)   "Lock-In" a favorable price to
        help him secure a loan.

The elements of improving market timing have already been discussed. A futures market trade can take the place of a forward cash market sale because it is easier and more convenient to execute, easier to reverse if market conditions change, or the only alternative available when cash market buyers are uninterested. In all of these cases, the real profit stems from the production operations. The futures market merely provides greater flexibility in reaping these profits at the most advantageous time.

Using the futures market to help secure a loan deserves special attention. Both the lending institution and the borrower need to understand the relationship between the loan account and the margin account.

A hedge is often used to help secure a loan. The producer can "lock-in" a favorable market price, assuming one is available and, thereby, guarantee a profitable operation. This reduction in risk may make an expansion loan more attractive to a lending institution. If the futures market is not offering a profitable price, this should help to serve as a check on any unreasonable price projections made by the producer. The futures market price should not dictate the decision by itself, but it does provide an extra input from an impartial source.

Once a loan is made in conjunction with a hedge, the lender should be willing to meet margin calls. The producer will have sold futures contracts to put on his hedge. If the market price moves up, he will sustain a loss in the futures market and will be asked to deposit more money in his margin account as it drops below the established call point. The lender must then furnish these extra funds or the broker will close out the hedge, leaving the producer as a speculator in the cash market. However, the lender should not be reluctant to do this. If the futures price increases, the cash market price should also increase. This means that the growing crop

47

against which the loan was made is now worth more in the
marketplace. The lending institution's increased contri-
bution to the margin account is merely commensurate with the
increased crop value.

If the cash market price should fall, the potential crop
value diminishes. At some point, the lender may feel that the
initial loan made on the higher price projection is in jeo-
pardy. He may then ask the producer to furnish extra collat-
eral. The producer can easily do this. When the cash market
price falls, the futures price should also fall accumulating
a profit against the selling hedge. The producer can draw
this profit from his margin account and give it to the lender.
He may draw out any profits as long as he does not reduce the
margin account below the original deposit. Where does this
money that he is drawing come from? The producer's profit is
equal to the loss sustained by the individual who bought his
contract. That individual is required to supplement his
original margin account to cover this loss. This provides the
money for the producer to draw against.

The important point to see here is that any profits which
accumulate in the margin account really belong to the lender.
The producer should not be allowed to use these funds for his
own purposes unless they are released by the lending institution.

5

TRADING TECHNIQUES FOR PRODUCERS

This chapter will focus on the use of the futures market
as a hedging tool. Carrying charges and basis movements will
be discussed in detail. However, as discussed in Chapter 1,
not every transaction made by a producer can be considered a
hedge. To illustrate this point, producer speculation will
also be discussed.

If a producer or processor could offset every crop or
inventory with a profitable cash market sale, there would be
no need for him to use a futures market. Of course, such
sales are not always possible. The crop may be in the field
and not ready for market when prices look favorable, there
may be no buyers available when the crop is ready for market,
or the going cash market price may be much lower than the
deferred delivery price. Under such circumstances, a hedge
may be used as a substitute for a cash market transaction.
The futures market loses much of its mystery when seen in this
light. This is an important point of view and is worth re-
stating in a slightly different way.

If a cash crop or cash inventory were to be offset with
a simultaneous cash market sale, the operator would be keenly
interested in the difference between his cost and sale price.
His profit comes from a favorable relationship between the two,
so naturally he sells to the buyer offering him the best
margin. These same considerations govern hedging transactions.
The producer looks for the cash crop-futures market combination
which reflects his best obtainable margin.

Let's consider a few examples to see how this works.

A Pre-Harvest Hedge

You will remember that our egg producer, in the previous
section, used the futures market to fix the price of a crop
not yet ready for market. A grain grower may do the same
thing. Consider a grain producer with a half-grown crop expected to yield a total of 10,000 bushels. He could wait
until harvest and sell at the going price. But it is now
April and the futures market price for August delivery is
$1.55 per bushel. He knows that the transportation and hand-
ling costs from the contract delivery point to his local
delivery point will be about 15 cents. That is, it would

cost him 15¢/bu. to transport his grain to the nearest
delivery point specified in the futures contract. This means
that the localized cash market equivalent price for his
August delivery is $1.55 − .15 = $1.40 per bushel. He likes
this price and fears that the local elevator will offer less
than $1.40 if he waits until his crop is harvested. He "puts
on" a hedge.

CASH MARKET		FUTURES MARKET
expects to produce 10,000 bu.	April	sells 10,000 bu. at $1.55

Assume that our producer is right and that demand is
lighter than the April market anticipated. He harvests his
crop in August and sells it to his local elevator at $1.10
per bushel. This price is 15 cents under the futures contract
price due to local transportation and handling charges. The
transaction looks like this:

CASH MARKET		FUTURES MARKET
Owns 10,000 bu.	April	sells 10,000 bu. at $1.55
sells 10,000 bu. at $1.10	August	buys 10,000 bu. at $1.25
		30¢/bu. profit

His net price is now $1.10 + .30 = $1.40 per bushel.
This was his original price objective. He was able to "lock-
in" the $1.40 price back in April and his net profit is now
the difference between this price and his actual cost per
bushel. If he had been wrong in guessing the price trend,
price might have been higher at harvest. In this case, a loss
in the futures market would bring his net price back down to
$1.40 per bushel.

We can now see that use of the futures market is a
management decision. It is not a device for obtaining an
inflated crop price each year. It is a device which offers
the producer maximum flexibility in accepting market prices
for his crop. It allows the marketing of a crop when no
local cash buyers are available, or are available, but at a
price less favorable than that offered by the futures market.

In our hedging examples so far, the basis determination has been deliberately avoided. The crops were growing and, therefore, no true cash price was given to use in calculating a basis. (You will recall that the basis is the difference between the cash and the futures price.) In addition, the crop was marketed during the contract month when the cash and futures prices come together for a zero basis. Let's see how basis calculations work by introducing another example.

A Storage Hedge

Assume we have a producer with on-farm storage facilities, the same producer as in our previous example. We will now assume that he has not yet sold his grain, but is just harvesting it in August. He is happy with the cash market price, but decides that he would like to carry the crop sale into a new tax year. He would also like to earn a storage fee to cover the use of his facilities. The first step is to close out his initial futures contract, which is expiring.

CASH MARKET		FUTURES MARKET
expects to produce 10,000 bu.	April	sells 10,000 bu. at $1.55
on hand 10,000 bu.	August	buys 10,000 bu. at $1.25
		30¢/bu. gain

Our producer still holds his cash crop which now may be assigned a market value. The local elevator price is $1.10 per bushel. He could speculate on a price rise by just holding the wheat. However, he is not interested in taking this risk. He sees that the January futures contract price is now $1.55 per bushel and decides to hedge his grain which he places in on-farm storage.

CASH MARKET		FUTURES MARKET
owns 10,000 bu. valued at $1.10	August	sells 10,000 bu. at $1.55

We should pause here to consider why the local basis is $1.55 − $1.10 = .45 per bushel at this time. There is a local transportation-handling charge of 15¢ per bushel so that the contract delivery point cash price is currently $1.10 + .15 =

51

$1.25 per bushel. In addition, it costs .05 per month in storage charges, interest on capital tied up, and insurance charges to store each bushel of the grain. From August to January is six months for a total carrying charge of 6 x .05 = 30¢ per bushel. The total price for January futures at the contract point may now be broken into its three components: $1.10 local cash price + .15 transportation charges + .30 carrying charges = $1.55 per bushel.

Assume that in December he decides to sell his grain and lift his hedge. The cash market price has gone up to $1.45 per bushel. We know that in December the January futures price will be $1.45 local cash price + .15 transportation charges + .05 storage for one month = $1.65 per bushel.

CASH MARKET		FUTURES MARKET
owns 10,000 bu. valued at $1.10	August	sells 10,000 bu. at $1.55
sells 10,000 bu. at $1.45	December	buys 10,000 bu. at $1.65
		.10 per bu. loss

Our producer has netted on his second hedge: $1.45/bu. cash sale - .10/bu. futures market loss - .25/bu. carrying charges for 5 months = $1.10 per bushel. He "locked-in" the August cash market price. His overall net from both hedges is now $1.10 net from second hedge + 30¢/bu. profit from the first hedge = $1.40/bushel. As you will recall, this is the localized cash market equivalent price that he "locked-in", way back in April.

What about the 25¢/bu. carrying charges which he must pay? Remember that his gross price from these two hedges is $1.45/bu. cash sale - 10¢/bu. loss from the second hedge + 30¢/bu. gain from the first hedge = $1.65 per bushel. He actually has enough money to cover his 25¢ cost and still net his $1.40 sale price. But where did this 25¢ come from? As always, carrying charges are reflected in the basis movement. The basis has narrowed from $1.55 - $1.10 = 45¢/bu., to $1.65 - $1.45 = 20¢/bu. That is, it has narrowed by 25¢ per bushel, exactly the amount of the carrying charges. The basis movement tends to extract the carrying charges from the longs in the commodity market. This is exactly what has happened here.

What if this same producer had decided to become part of the 1 percent who actually deliver against their contracts? Would he be better off or worse off?

Futures Market Delivery

In order to deliver, he must hold his contract into January. Assume, for ease of calculation, that he holds it until the actual expiration date when the basis becomes zero. Further assume that delivery looks attractive against a cash market price which falls to $1.50 at the contract delivery point. At a zero basis, this means that the futures market price is also $1.50. The local cash market price in the producing area must be $1.50/bu. − .15/bu. transportation charges = $1.35 per bushel. The situation looks like this:

CASH MARKET		FUTURES MARKET
owns grain valued at $1.10	August	sells contracts at $1.55
owns grain valued at $1.35	January	market price stands at $1.50

Now delivery would appear to be attractive. Our producer owns grain valued at $1.35/bu., but he can deliver against his futures market sale and receive $1.55/bu. He delivers and receives a gross price of $1.55/bu. − .15 transportation charges + .30/bu. profit from his first hedge = $1.70 per bushel. But remember, that the producer stored his crop from August to January. Six months storage at 5¢ per month cost him a total of 30¢ per bushel. His net price is then: $1.70/bu. − .30/bu. = $1.40 per bushel. In an orderly market, a producer is indifferent as to whether he makes an offsetting trade or actually delivers. In this case, he netted $1.40 per bushel either way.

We have now seen two uses made of the futures market: (1) to "fix" the price of growing crop, and (2) to "fix" the price of a crop held in storage space. Another use may be illustrated with a slightly different situation.

Producer Speculation

Consider a neighbor of our producer from the previous example. He, too, has just harvested his grain crop, but does not have any storage facilities. Although he must sell his crop, he regrets the decision because he feels that the cash price is going to rise. Since he would be willing to speculate on the cash crop, but cannot, he substitutes a futures market speculation.

FUTURES MARKET
August

buys 10,000 bu.
at $1.55

Of course, we already know what happened to price. He pulls out of the market in December with the following results:

FUTURES MARKET
August

buys 10,000 bu.
at $1.55

December

sells 10,000 bu.
at $1.65

.10 per bu. profit

Our speculator has gained 10 cents per bushel.[5] But we know that the cash market price moved from $1.10/bu. to $1.45/bu. over this period and, therefore, he could have gained 35¢/bu. by speculating in the cash market alone. Why the difference? Remember that whoever is long in the futures market generally forfeits the storage charges. These charges amount to 25¢ per bushel for the five months, exactly the difference between the cash market speculation and the futures market speculation.

One more use of the futures market needs to be examined: to establish the cost of a commodity to be purchased later.

Hedging Future Inventory Requirements

Suppose we have a livestock producer who would like to fill his yearly grain requirements at the August harvest price of $1.10 per bushel, but he lacks the storage space. He decides to hedge his future purchase with a January futures

----

[5] In all of these examples, a brokerage fee should be deducted. The fee is small, and it has been neglected to keep the calculations as simple as possible.

contract.

CASH MARKET		FUTURES MARKET
will need 15,000 bu.	August	buys 15,000 bu. at $1.55

In December he actually purchases his grain and lifts his hedge.

CASH MARKET		FUTURES MARKET
buys 15,000 bu.	December	sells 15,000 bu. at $1.65
		.10 per bu. gain

His net feed cost is now $1.45 − .10 = $1.35 per bushel. If he had been able to purchase his grain in December at $1.10, he would have had to store it for five months at a cost of 5¢ per month. By December, he would have had $1.10 + .25 = $1.35 invested. His hedge worked perfectly.

We have now seen four uses of the futures market by producers:

(1) to "fix" the price of growing crop for later sale,

(2) to "fix" the price of a crop in storage and earn a payment for the storage space,

(3) to substitute a futures market speculation for a desirable, but unavailable, cash market speculation, and

(4) to "fix" the price of feed for later purchase.

Uses 1 and 2 are called selling hedges. Use 4 is called a buying hedge.

Potential Problems

The examples used were not the typical textbook examples where the basis never changes. You have been exposed to the fundamentals of basis movement. However, it must be pointed out that actual hedges do not always work just like the ones in this section. There are several reasons for this; the more obvious will be dealt with first.

    a. Futures market contracts are not written for every month of the year. Therefore, there may not be a contract month in your crop year which expires later than your final cash market transaction. If this is the case, you would be forced to lift your hedge before the cash market transactions are completed.

    b. Not all grades of commodity are traded under a futures contract. Your cash commodity may not be a grade represented in the futures market. If this is so, slight differences may occur in the cash-futures price fluctuation pattern.

    c. Futures contracts are traded in standard volume multiples. You may have to select a contract number which leaves part of your cash crop unhedged or purchase one additional contract and overhedge your position.

    d. The price pattern at your local delivery point may differ slightly from the price pattern at the contract delivery point. With the trend away from centralized markets and toward country contract delivery points, this factor becomes less important.

    e. It is possible to have trouble lifting your hedge. Standard price fluctuation limits are established by the commodity exchanges and the day's trading is suspended if price exceeds these limits. This is a rare occurrence.

    f. Your commodity may not be traded on any future exchange. It is possible to hedge with a similar commodity if one exists. The classic example is: The corn futures market is a good hedge for raw mash, a bad hedge for whiskey, and a terrible hedge for 12-year old bourbon.

g. The basis often will not become exactly
   zero at delivery time. Futures market
   delivery is generally more inconvenient
   than cash market delivery and may incur
   extra handling charges. In the cash
   market, the buyer can discover exactly
   what quality he will receive, exactly
   when he will receive it, and exactly
   where delivery will take place. In the
   futures market, some uncertainty exists
   for all of these items because cash
   market product and product delivered on
   the futures market are not really perfect substitutes; some price difference
   may exist at the contract expiration.

One final source of difficulty remains. The definition
of basis used in this section included storage charges, insurance fees, and interest on the invested capital. However,
trader expectations also influence the basis. If conditions
are expected to influence futures markets differently than
they influence the current cash market, the basis may deviate
from the normal pattern.

It should now be clear just what a hedge can and cannot
do. It cannot provide complete price protection. It can,
however, trade the large risk of price fluctuation for the
smaller risk of basis abnormality. In most markets, the
basis will not be a perfect reflection of carrying charges.
A broker can provide valuable advice on historical and expected basis patterns.

Inverted Markets

Occasionally, cash market prices will be greater than
futures market prices. Such a market is said to be inverted
since the carrying charges have become negative; the market
is "upside down". This condition is an example of expectations becoming important enough to dominate the market. For
example, if there is a shortage of cash crop available for
immediate use, and if there is a large crop in the field
nearing harvest time, the market may invert. The current
shortage drives the cash price very high, while the expectation of a large future harvest holds futures prices down.

This condition is expected to be short-run in nature,
with the markets returning to their normal relationship when
the special situation has passed. This condition causes

special problems for hedgers. In order for the market to return to its normal relationship, the futures market price must rise relative to the cash market. A selling hedge is, therefore, less favorable than if the market were not inverted. As the futures market rises and the cash market falls, the hedger loses in both markets until the prices reach their normal relationship and the hedge becomes effective. Such a market may provide some price protection in a hedge, but its effectiveness is reduced.

A buying hedge, however, becomes more favorable than if the market were not inverted. As the futures market rises and the cash market falls, the buying hedge profits in both markets until the prices reach their normal relationship.

A commodity broker should be consulted before hedging into an inverted market. He can give advice in light of the special situation causing the inversion.

6

MARKET ANALYSIS

Successful futures trading requires careful market analysis for hedgers and speculators alike. The market conditions are constantly changing and there are no automatic formulas which guarantee success. The vigilance required of speculators is very expensive in terms of time, although a hedger can escape with a smaller time investment. If the commodity market could deliver one message loud and clear, to all new traders, it would be this: There is no mercy for the idle dabbler in the commodity market.

This chapter will discuss the basic principles of market analysis. The discussion is necessarily brief since a complete treatment would require several volumes for this topic alone. Readers interested in pursuing this subject are referred to the list of additional readings at the end of this book.

The First Step

The first step in establishing a market position is a review of the farming operation. The farmer must establish a set of objectives for futures trading activity consistent with his overall productive operation. It is essential that he enter the market with a plan of operation firmly in mind. Changing conditions constantly buffet the trader from all sides and only a clear set of objectives will keep him on the right track. This point is overlooked by many people who soon find themselves so immersed in the day-to-day price fluctuations that they lose sight of their overall goal. Rapid in-and-out trading (reversals of position) is the surest way for the nonprofessional to establish a losing record. Of course, the trader can change his mind. But he should do so only when a major market change is underway. It is best to leave rapid-fire day trading to the professionals.

One legitimate objective for a producer would be to improve his market timing. A trader with this in mind would think of a futures transaction as a substitute for a cash market sale, either on-the-spot market, or through a forward pricing arrangement, for his commodity. He would be interested in taking only a few positions each year when he feels that prices are about to decline. Since he would not buy and sell his cash commodity daily, he is not interested in buying and selling futures contracts daily. He is basically a producer, and he trades on the futures market in a pattern consistent with his crop cycle. Other producer objectives were discussed in Chapter 4.

Once the basic objectives are firmly in mind, a conference with a reliable broker is in order. He can provide a quick overview of the current market situation and highlight any future events which are likely to occur. A word of caution should be added here. The broker provides valuable advice, but the final decision rests with the individual trader. Futures market trading is a management decision which must be made with an eye to the overall farming operation. Only the owner, not the broker, has the necessary perspective for a decision of this kind.

Other relevant sources of information would also be reviewed by the hedger at this time. Several likely sources were listed at the end of Chapter 1.

Fundamental Versus Technical Analysis

Once the basic information is at hand, there are two general methods of analysis: fundamental and technical. These are not mutually exclusive techniques, but the proponents of each have a strong tendency to divide into hostile camps. A fundamentalist keeps his eyes on the facts. He analyzes the basic supply and demand conditions for the commodity in question. The technician avoids the fundamentals entirely and watches price movement patterns instead. He reasons that all factors influencing a commodity are reflected in its price and, therefore, the best way to detect trends is to watch price movements. You can see how these two methods would tend to attract individuals with different temperaments.

Skillful fundamental analysis requires sound common sense and the ability to evaluate the future impact of events. These particular skills come from trading experience and a good working knowledge of the commodity involved. The fundamentalist is likely to locate major long-term trends in the movement of prices. However, it is difficult to predict exactly when these trends will get underway. It takes margin money and the courage of conviction for a fundamentalist to hold his position until his predictions are vindicated. His position may be a lonely one for quite some time since he typically enters the market before his anticipated trend is clearly underway. One further problem plagues the fundamentalist. It seems that no two people ever reach exactly the same conclusion when confronted with the same information on supply and demand. Bulls (those convinced that price is moving up) and bears (those convinced it is moving down) often read the same news with equal conviction that it confirms their original analysis. You can now appreciate the fact that this type of analysis cannot be learned from a simple set of rules. It must be developed over time with actual trading experience. Your paper trading exercise is designed to help you acquire this experience as painlessly as possible.

Skillful technical analysis tends to keep a trader "running with the crowd". Since price movements themselves trigger trading decisions, trends are already underway before the technician reacts. He will not generally catch a trend as early, nor ride it as long, as a fundamentalist. But neither will he tolerate large paper losses while waiting for the market to come around to his point of view.

There are many, many individual chart techniques which are used by technicians. Only one of these will be presented here as an illustration of the type of analysis which may be used.

A bar chart is the basic tool of the technician. Each day's trading is recorded on a chart with a vertical bar representing the price range for that day and a small horizontal crossbar representing the closing price. Such a chart is illustrated below:

Figure 9.

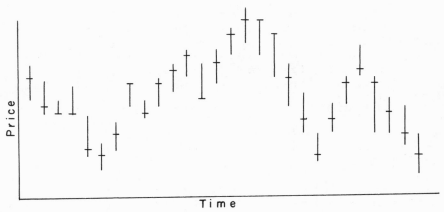

A 30-day or 90-day moving average may be charted on the same graph. The moving average price represents the average of the closing prices for a designated number of days extending into the past. The actual calculation will be illustrated with a 5-day moving average. Assume the following 7-day series of closing prices: $2.00, $3.00, $4.00, $5.00, $4.00, $6.00, and $8.00. A 5-day moving average represents an average of the closing prices for the last five days. It is calculated by starting with the current day's price, adding the last four daily prices, and dividing by 5. The result is graphed on the same vertical line as the current day's price. This calculation is illustrated below.

Closing Prices	Work Column	Moving Average
$2.00		
3.00		
4.00		
5.00		
4.00	18 ÷ 5 =	3.6
6.00	22 ÷ 5 =	4.4
8.00	27 ÷ 5 =	5.4

The first four days in a 5-day moving average series will not have an average calculated since there are not enough prices with which to construct the average. Each day after the fifth, the current day's price will be added, and the price from five days ago will be dropped. This process insures that there will always be exactly five days in the average.

The moving average is a smoothing process which helps prevent getting lost in day-to-day fluctuations and losing sight of the long-term trend. When a daily price bar breaks through the moving average line, a trading signal is flashed. If price breaks through from below the moving average, it is a buy signal; if it breaks through from above, it is a sell signal.

Figure 10.

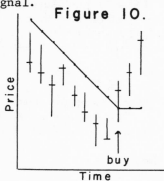

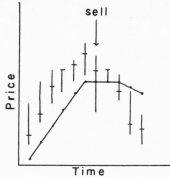

When prices are moving in a downward trend, the moving average will always remain above the daily closing prices. When price breaks up through the average line, it is a sign that the down trend is reversing. When prices are moving in an upward trend, the moving average will always remain below the daily closing prices. A trend reversal is signaled when the daily price line breaks down through the average line.

Since the purpose of a moving average is to depict long-term trends, a 5-day average would be much too short for practical use. A 30, 60, or 90-day average would be more appropriate. Many, many other technical chart formations are in use today. To name just a few: head and shoulders, inverted head and shoulders, saucers, flags, pennants, wedges, double tops, single-day island reversals, break-away gaps, and exhaustion gaps. One reference for further information on this subject is:

> Jiler, H., ed., Guide to Commodity Price Forecasting, Commodity Research Bureau, Inc., New York, 1965.

Technical analysis seems attractive to many market newcomers because of its formalized trading rules. It seems so much more objective than fundamental analysis. This is not the case. Chart formations are often difficult to recognize and subject to individual interpretation. At times, this can be like looking at an ink blot test and trying to find the hidden meaning in each formation. Neither technique is simple, nor fast, and there is no substitute for experience and good common sense. You should choose the method or combination of methods which fit your own personality and which you feel comfortable with. A hedger will probably use fundamental analysis as his basic tool with technical advice from his broker as to the best timing to take his positions. In other words, the producer will use supply and demand analysis, coupled with his crop production cycle, to decide whether he should buy or sell commodity futures. He will then ask his broker if the technical factors give any indication as to whether he should take his position right away or wait for a more favorable technical condition before making his trade.

Account Analysis and Trading Techniques

Market analysis is, of course, a very important aspect of hedging. Recall that the easiest way for a producer to decide whether or not to hedge is for him to ask the question: What am I afraid of? If he is growing a crop for sale and he is afraid of a price decline, he would protect himself with a selling hedge. If he is a livestock producer and he is afraid that the price of his feed is going up, he would protect himself with a buying hedge. If the producer feels that the impending price movement will be favorable to him, then he has nothing to fear and he would not hedge. However, there is another type of analysis which a hedger must worry about: account analysis.

It is very easy for a hedger, especially a new hedger, to lose sight of his original trading plan and start speculating in the market. There are a few techniques of account management which can help to overcome this tendency. The balance of this chapter will discuss these techniques.

It is most unsettling for a new hedger to receive his first margin call. When his broker telephones to ask for more money, the producer tends to lose all sight of his original goals and think only of his losses in the futures market. As a result, he will often close out his contract without any re-evaluation of the reasons for establishing the original hedge. It is difficult to remain rational when the margin call rears its ugly head. A new hedger would be well-advised to overmargin for at least a few trades. He would put up more margin than required by the broker, $800 instead of $600, for example. If the market moves against his futures position, this extra margin gives him a little extra time to re-evaluate his hedge before a margin call forces a decision. If market conditions have changed, the hedge may well merit closing out. If conditions have not changed, a hedge should not be closed out simply because of a margin call.

Another device may be used to help a producer decide whether or not to close out his hedge before his cash market transaction is completed. A daily or weekly record book should be set up to show both cash market prices and futures market prices. Once a hedge is placed, the producer begins to think only of his gains or losses in the futures market. The real issue is how well the total hedge is working. Losses in the futures market may not be disturbing if they are more than offset by gains in the cash market. This is easiest to see if a record is established to reflect both sides of the hedge.

Account analysis brings up the question: How much of the crop should be hedged to start with? That is, how large should the account be, relative to the cash crop? As a rule, the only true hedges in the textbook sense are those used to secure a financial loan. These hedges may be established for the full crop and held until the actual cash market sale. Most hedges not used to secure a loan will be made initially for less than the full crop volume. A hedger might, for example, sell futures contracts equivalent to one-half his cash crop volume. He would then watch the market for price movement. If the market moves against his cash market position, the hedge will be scaled up. If the price movement is favorable to his cash market position, the hedge will gradually be lifted. In each case, the hedger should not trade on price movement alone. He should use price movement to signal when he should re-evaluate his initial decision. If a price decline on a selling hedge helps to confirm the hedger's market analysis, he will increase his hedge. If a price increase on a selling hedge signals that market conditions have changed, the hedge should be modified accordingly. One of the real advantages of hedging is that it allows a position reversal if actual market conditions change. Once a forward pricing contract is negotiated in the cash market, the seller is locked in, regardless of any changes in supply and demand.

Some brokers will encourage an initial position equal to 25 percent or less of the cash crop volume. However, taking a position this small forces the producer to watch the market very closely, being constantly ready to scale his hedge up or down. This may encourage the rapid in-and-out trading which may be appropriate for a speculator, but not for a hedger. A hedger must avoid trading on price movement alone.

Trading Rules

A few basic trading rules should be followed regardless of the method of market analysis. These particular rules are no guarantee of a profit, but they should help to prevent major losses from accumulating.

1. Use stop orders when the cash market appears to be very favorable. Producers are notorious optimists and feel that when prices are good they will surely get better. As a result, they are least likely to hedge when it would be most beneficial for them to do so. When prices are high, place a stop order below the current market price. If the market should suddenly turn around, the stop will be activated, and a hedge will be placed close to the market top. If the price should continue to increase, the

stop may be moved up along with the market.[6]

This technique will help producers to deal with their optimism. However, they must remember to cancel their old stops when a new one is placed, or when the cash crop is sold. If they do not, a forgotten stop may be activated at an inappropriate time.

2. Use market orders to close out futures positions. The more sophisticated types of orders are fine for entering the market, but they may not be flexible enough to close out a position quickly. A major unfavorable price move may start while the trader is holding out for those last few pennies of profit.

3. Always keep the size of the futures market position small enough to feel comfortable with. Each hedger must judge this for himself. In other words, never become so committed financially that trading becomes emotional. A hedger must be able to stick to a rational plan of action consistent with his long-term goals. Some people are not emotionally equipped to do this and these people should not trade on the futures market.

4. Do not be afraid to re-evaluate a market position. Conditions do change and any new market information should be carefully considered. When a hedger is on the wrong side of the market, he must have the wisdom to take a small loss before it builds into a large one.

5. Do not feel that a hedge should be placed routinely. A hedge should be established only when a producer feels that he needs price protection. When prices are improving, a hedge is not desirable, although a stop

_____

[6] The question of how far below the market to place a stop order is not easily answered. This depends to a large extent on the volatility of the particular contract being traded. A good broker can provide the best advice on this subject.

order may be appropriate to guard against
market reversals.

6. Do not rely exclusively on chart formations,
    and do not interpret chart patterns without
    a good historical record for that commodity.
    All chart movements are relative and should
    be evaluated in light of the previous actions
    of the same commodity.

7. Never "average down" to recover losses.
    Many traders respond to a move against
    them by increasing the size of their
    position. They reason that the market must
    eventually reverse itself and that when it
    does, they will be able to recover all of
    their losses. However, a commodity con-
    tract may close out without reversing it-
    self resulting in very large losses from
    this averaging down technique. If a
    trader concludes that his initial market
    evaluation was wrong, he must take his
    loss while it is still small.

And, finally, remember the words of John Meynard Keynes:

> "There is nothing so disastrous
> as a rational investment policy
> in an irrational world."

At times, the market may indeed seem to you to be acting
irrationally. If this is the case, it usually indicates a
lack of "feel" for the market which causes uneasiness with
your basic trading plan. This is the signal to pull out of
the market. Just as you should never enter the market without a plan of action firmly in mind, neither should you continue trading when you feel that plan is failing you. Never
try to second guess yourself while trading.

APPENDIX

COST OF PRODUCTION: AN ELUSIVE CONCEPT

WRITTEN BY

A. GENE NELSON
Assistant Professor
Department of Agricultural Economics
Oregon State University
Corvallis

This section provides a brief insight into the
difficulties associated with determining the
cost of production associated with a particular
crop. The material is designed for presentation
by a group leader and to stimulate discussion.
It may be used outside of a group workshop as
an introduction to the relevant concepts which
will serve as the base for further readings.

Cost of Production: An Elusive Concept

To make effective use of the futures market, the producer must know his "cost of production" for the commodity involved. Financial advisors, including brokers and lenders, can provide valuable counsel on the general advisability of hedging given the market climate. It is up to the producer, however, to determine the target price at which he will hedge. This target price should be based on his cost of production with possibly a margin for profit. Any hedge placed below the cost "locks in" a loss, not a profit. While a producer may hedge at a target price lower than his cost in order to minimize his loss due to a serious price decline, this policy cannot be pursued in the long run. If faced with this prospect, the producer should critically review his farm organization and alternatives.

Previous material has discussed the mechanics and considerations involved in using the futures market. This section will attempt to answer the questions of what a cost is, how it is measured, and which costs are relevant in determining a target price. The concepts and principles involved in determining that "elusive cost of production" will be presented.

The Measurement of Cost

Few managers agree on what should be included in the "cost of production". Even if they do agree on _what_ should be included, there is seldom agreement on _how_ it should be measured. This lack of an understanding is understandable. Estimating production costs is a difficult process complicated by variations in the resources available and in the production situation. This variation exists both between farms and between time periods.

A cost may be defined as a charge made for a resource used in the production of a commodity. Not just one cost item must be considered, but a large number of individual cost items must be evaluated. A partial list might include land, seed, fertilizer, fuel, labor, and chemicals. The composite of cost items required to produce a commodity is referred to as the "cost of production" for that commodity.

These charges or cost items can be measured according to at least three points of view. From the accountant's viewpoint, costs are outlays that arise from the production process. They consist of explicit payments for resources bought outright or hired by the farm business. The farm's payroll, payments for fertilizer and chemicals, expenses for overhead items of various kinds, and depreciation allowances are examples of costs as listed by the accountant.

The economist, on the other hand, measures costs implicitly. He argues that the accountant's measurement of cost is for purposes other than decision-making and, therefore, overlooks the costs of self-owned, self-employed resources. Value of labor contributed by the farmer and interest on his equity capital are examples of costs often excluded by accountants. The economist measures cost of production for a particular commodity as the foregone returns that resources used in its production could have earned elsewhere.[7] This is the opportunity cost principle.

Estimating the opportunity cost of a resource is illustrated in the following examples:

(1) The opportunity cost of the time the farmer puts into his own business is the salary he could earn in his best alternative employment.

(2) The opportunity cost of the equity capital invested in the farm business is the interest that could be earned on these funds invested in the best alternative venture.

(3) The opportunity cost of using land to produce one crop is the sacrifice of returns that would be possible from another crop.

(4) The opportunity cost of using land that would otherwise be idle is nil since its use requires no sacrifice of other opportunities.

It follows from the above that opportunity costs require the measurement of sacrifices, that is, foregone returns. If a decision to produce involves no sacrifices, it is cost free. The expenditure of cash involves a sacrifice of other possible expenditures, and, therefore, is an opportunity cost. Under

---

[7] Leftwich, Richard H. The Price System and Resource Allocation, 3rd ed., Holt, Rinehart, and Winston, New York, 1966. Chapter 8.

this principle, the only costs that are relevant for decision-making are opportunity costs.

The third point of view regarding the cost of production is that of the financier. His concern is that the process of production will generate sufficient cash to maintain the liquidity of the farm business. He is concerned that the cash flow will be available not only to meet expenses for fertilizer, land taxes, chemicals, etc., but also to meet principal and interest obligations, to pay income taxes, and to provide for family living expenses.

The Dichotomies of Cost

There are a number of ways to classify and examine costs. Each of these methods adds something to understanding the principles of measuring costs. The classification of individual cost items is somewhat arbitrary. Some items could fall into one classification under certain circumstances and into another classification under different circumstances. The producer must determine how the items should be classified for his particular situation.

Fixed Versus Variable Costs. Variable costs are the costs which vary with the volume of product produced in a given period of time. Costs of seed, fuel, and fertilizer are examples of variable costs in crop production. Fixed costs are those which do not change with the level of output, that is, they remain constant. Taxes on land and buildings; interest on the investment in land, buildings, and machinery; and depreciation on buildings and machinery are typical examples of fixed costs.[8]

Avoidable Versus Non-Avoidable Costs. Another useful cost classification is based on the manager's control over the cost item. An avoidable cost is any cost that can be eliminated by an appropriate decision. For example, if ceasing grain production means the combine can be sold, then the costs associated with owning and operating the combine are avoidable. On the other hand, the overhead cost for the farm shop is non-avoidable assuming that the farm business is to continue. The

---

[8] Castle, Emery N., Manning H. Becker, and Frederick J. Smith, Farm Business Management: The Decision-Making Process, 2nd ed., The Macmillan Co., New York, 1972, pp. 28-32, 86-91.

measurement of avoidable costs includes variable costs plus external opportunity costs.[9]

Implicit Versus Explicit Costs. Explicit costs are those that are recognized in the account books, as would be true of payments for materials and supplies and for hired labor. Implicit (or imputed) costs are the opportunity costs that are not recorded by the accountant. The opportunity cost of using a resource is the return that could be received from that resource used in its best alternative.

Cash Versus Non-Cash Costs. Cash payments made outside the farm business for fuel, fertilizer, feed, and similar items are frequently referred to "out-of-pocket costs". Other cash transactions include capital purchases, principal payments, income taxes, and family living. Although it may be a misnomer to call these costs, it is important to recognize that the production process must generate sufficient cash flow to meet all these obligations. The non-cash costs such as operator labor, depreciation, and interest on equity capital do not involve cash payments.

The Cost Depends On The Situation

The cost of production is a "perishable" product. It varies over time and between farms. This variation is due not only to differences in farm size, land prices, productivity, etc., but also to differences in the alternatives the farmer is able and/or willing to consider. It is the differences in these alternatives that indicates the applicability of the various approaches to classifying costs presented above. The appropriate dichotomy depends on the alternatives the manager has available.

To illustrate the application of these cost classification concepts, five case situations will be analyzed. Each of the five situations will be based on the same set of physical farm resources. The only differences will be the alternatives considered by the manager in each case.

The farm is a grain enterprise with 1,000 acres harvested annually. The yield is 40 bushels per acre, and the value of

---

[9] Goldschmidt, Yaagov. Information for Management Decisions: A System for Economic Analysis and Accounting Procedures, Cornell University Press, Ithaca, New York, 1970. Chapter V.

land is $400 per harvested acre. The "direct crop expenses" for seed, fertilizer, chemicals, fuel, machine repair, hired seasonal labor, and operating capital interest amount to $15 per acre harvested. These assumptions will apply for each of the five following cases.

The Full Cost Case. Frank believes he must recover "full economic costs" from the use of all his resources in grain production. If grain production does not provide this level of returns, he will divert the resources to other uses that will. For example, he considers that he could sell his land at the $400 figure and invest the proceeds at 6% interest. Taxes amount to another $7 which must be recovered. If he cannot earn the $6 to offset depreciation and taxes on machinery, he would sell it and invest the money elsewhere. He also puts a charge of $2 per acre on his labor, accounting for his opportunities in other employment. Frank's costs total to $56 per acre of grain produced. This amounts to $1.40 per bushel.

"Full-Cost Frank"

Land taxes and interest....................$31.00
Direct crop expenses...................... 15.00
Machine depreciation, interest, taxes..... 6.00
Operator's Labor.......................... 2.00
General overhead.......................... 2.00

Cost Per Acre of Grain...............$56.00

Cost Per Bushel of Grain............$ 1.40

The Variable Cost Case. Virgil has determined that based on his analysis of the long-run prospects in agriculture, he will not consider selling off his resource base. Therefore, the costs he needs to cover include only those that vary with the level of output. If he produces grain, he will incur the $15 cost for the direct crop expenses. Although depreciation is often considered a fixed cost, Virgil feels that if he did not produce grain, the reduced wear and tear on the machinery would decrease the depreciation by $1 per acre.[10/] Virgil's cost per acre of grain produced is $16, or 40¢ per bushel.

_____

[10/] Depreciation can be thought of as consisting of fixed and variable components. The fixed component results from obsolescence and wear and tear determines the variable component.

"Variable-Cost Virgil"

```
Direct crop expenses.....................$15.00
Machine depreciation (variable)...........  1.00

   Cost Per Acre of Grain...............$16.00

   Cost Per Bushel of Grain............$  .40
```

The Avoidable Cost Case. In determining his cost of producing grain, Alfred will not consider selling his farm and believes his primary alternative is to rent it to a neighbor. He expects that this lease would return $19 per acre. With this alternative, he could also avoid the $15 charge for direct crop expenses and he could sell his machinery to avoid depreciation, interest, and taxes of $6. As Alfred's employment opportunities are very limited, he cannot avoid the cost for operator labor. Alfred's cost is $40 per acre and $1 per bushel of grain produced.

"Avoidable-Cost Alfred"

```
Land rental return........................$19.00
Direct Crop expenses......................  15.00
Machine depreciation, interest, taxes.....   6.00

   Cost Per Acre of Grain...............$40.00

   Cost Per Bushel of Grain.............$ 1.00
```

The Opportunity Cost Case. Oscar's best alternative, in lieu of using his resources to produce grain, is to grow another crop selling at $43 per acre. Thus, Oscar's costs for producing grain include the direct crop expenses of $15. To this cost for grain, he adds the difference between the value of his alternative crop and the direct expenses for producing this crop. His cost per acre becomes $42 or $1.05 per bushel of grain produced.

"Opportunity-Cost Oscar"

```
Direct crop expenses for grain............$15.00
Plus:  Alternative crop sales.............  43.00
Direct expenses for alternative crop......-16.00

   Cost Per Acre of Grain...............$42.00

   Cost Per Bushel of Grain.............$ 1.05
```

The Cash Cost Case. Carl is concerned that he has enough cash available at the end of the year to meet all his obligations. He has no sources of cash outside the farm business. Therefore, the production of grain must generate the cash to cover all his cash costs plus provide for principal payments, income and self-employment taxes, and family living expenses. Twenty-five dollars is required to meet the principal and interest payments on his land plus pay property taxes. He also has debt outstanding on his farm machinery, which requires $4 for principal, interest, and taxes. His general overhead expenses include $1 which is a cash payment. Carl's total cash "cost" then is $52 per acre and $1.30 per bushel.

"Cash-Cost Carl"

Land principal, interest, and taxes.......$25.00
Direct crop expenses...................... 15.00
Machine principal, interest, and taxes.... 4.00
General overhead (cash)................... 1.00
Family living expenses.................... 5.00
Income and self-employment taxes.......... 2.00

Cost Per Acre of Grain...............$52.00

Cost Per Bushel of Grain.............$ 1.30

Comparing the Cases. Despite having the same productivity (40 bushels per acre), the same land value ($400 per acre), and the same direct crop expenses ($15 per acre); the range in the "cost of production" is from 40¢ per bushel to $1.40, as summarized below:

Situation	Cost/Bushel
"Full-Cost Frank".....................	$1.40
"Variable-Cost Virgil"................	0.40
"Avoidable-Cost Alfred"...............	1.00
"Opportunity-Cost Oscar"..............	1.05
"Cash-Cost Carl"......................	1.30

The difference is due to the alternative the manager has available. Is he willing to sell out like Frank? Or, does he wish to maintain his present resource base like Virgil? Would he consider renting the land out like Alfred? Or, is another crop the best alternative, as it is for Oscar? If cash flow is the critical consideration, then the situation is the same as Carl's.

In summary, that which is actually given up to produce grain depends on the alternatives the manager is willing and able to consider and those costs he needs to recover through the production process. Thus, any estimate of the cost of production must be made on a situation basis, depending, at any point in time, on alternatives of the producer himself, as well as his resources.

Concluding Remarks

The purpose here has been to explore the various concepts of cost as they relate to estimating the "cost of production" for a commodity. Knowing the cost of production is necessary not only to make effective use of the futures market but also to decision-making regarding the organization and operation of the farm business.

Two principles emerge as central issues in the estimation of cost. The first is the principle of opportunity cost, that is, the return foregone by not allocating the resource to an alternative use. The second principle is that the opportunity cost depends on what the manager, given his particular situation, is willing and able to consider as an alternative use of the resource.

The result of applying these principles is a large variation in cost between farms and over time. The cost of production, thus, becomes a question that each producer must answer for himself after a critical examination of his situation and his alternatives. Only in this way can he be certain that the cost is relevant to the decisions he must make.

SUGGESTED FURTHER READINGS

The material in this text was adopted from many sources. The author wishes to acknowledge the following sources and to provide a list of additional readings for those wishing to pursue this topic.

Arthur, H. B. Commodity Futures As a Business Management Tool, Harvard University Press, Boston, 1971.

Bakken, H. H. Futures Trading in Livestock, Mimir Publishers, Inc., Madison, Wisconsin, 1970.

Board of Trade of the City of Chicago. Commodity Training Manual, Belveal and Company, Wilmette, Illinois, 1966.

Board of Trade of the City of Chicago. Understanding and Using the Commodity Futures Market, Chicago, undated.

Gold, G. Modern Commodity Futures Trading, Commodity Research Bureau, Inc., New York, 1971.

Hieronymus, T. A. Economics of Futures Trading, Commodity Research Bureau, Inc., New York, 1971.

Jiler, H., ed. Guide to Commodity Price Forecasting, Commodity Research Bureau, Inc., New York, 1965.

GLOSSARY

Afloat   Grain which is in storage on the water. Usually in the holds of ships at anchor.

Asked   The price at which sellers will trade. This is usually accompanied by a bid, the price which buyers are willing to pay. The bid price is often a better indication of the true market level.

Average Down To increase the size of a market position as it accumulates losses. The hope is to recover all losses if the price trend should reverse.

Basis   The futures market price minus the cash market price for a particular commodity contract. The term "local basis" is sometimes used to indicate the difference between local market prices and terminal market prices.

Bear   A trader or market analyst who feels that prices will decline.

Bid   The price at which buyers will trade. This is usually accompanied by an ask, the price at which sellers will trade. The bid price is often a better indication of the true market level.

Board Order A standing order to execute a transaction at a specified price or one more favorable to the customer. Also called a Market If Touched Order.

Break   A sharp price movement. A market may "break upward" or "break downward", although the term is reserved by some for price declines.

Broker   An agent for the customer who takes charge of executing an order, usually charging a commission for his services.

Bulge   A large price rise.

Bull   A trader or market analyst who feels that prices will rise.

Buying Hedge A short position in the cash market hedged by a long position in the futures market.

Call Point The price at which the margin account reaches its maintenance level and the customer is asked to put up more money.

Carrying Charges The costs of storing the cash commodity. These charges include the physical storage costs, insurance costs, and an opportunity cost for the interest lost on the money tied up in the commodity.

Clearing House That branch of the Commodity Exchange which records and supervises all trading accounts and futures market deliveries.

Commission The broker's fee for executing a trade. In the commodity market, commissions are round-trip, entitling the trader to buy and sell his contract. The fee is paid only once after the initial position is closed out.

Commodity Exchange A non-profit organization which supervises and facilitates trading activity.

Contract The standard trading unit for the commodity in question. Each contract also specifies at a minimum the acceptable grades, acceptable delivery points, and the contract expiration date.

Cover To close out a position previously taken, usually by buying to cover a previous short position. See also *Liquidate*.

Day Order An order which expires at the end of the day's trading.

Deferred Delivery Any contract month beyond the current delivery month. See also *Nearby Delivery*.

Delivery Month The month in which the futures contract expires and any outstanding contracts come due for delivery.

Delivery Notice   A notice given by the seller of a futures contract of his intent to deliver the cash commodity. This notice is passed on by the Commodity Clearing House to a buyer who must accept delivery or retainder.

Delivery Points   The contract specified locations at which the cash commodity may be delivered to satisfy a futures contract.

Floor Broker   A broker authorized by the Commodity Exchange to trade in the commodity pit for the account of others.

Floor Trader   An exchange member authorized by the Commodity Exchange to trade in the commodity pit for his own account.

Hedging   The process of offsetting an existing risk by taking an opposite position on another risk likely to move in the same direction. See also *Buying Hedge* and *Selling Hedge*.

Inverted Market   A market in which the cash market price is greater than the futures market price. The basis is negative.

Late Tape   A lag in the reporting of futures market prices due to unusually heavy trading.

Leg   A sizeable price movement which is relatively uninterrupted by any corrections or reversals.

Leverage   The control of a large asset with a small down payment. A small percentage change in the total asset price then represents a very large change in the small amount of invested capital.

Life of Contract   The period between the beginning of trading in a specific delivery month until the expiration date for that contract month. The market itself determines when there is enough interest to begin trading specific months.

Limit Move A price advance or decline which is sufficiently above or below the previous day's closing price to cause the Exchange to suspend trading in that delivery month. Each commodity contract has stated limits which trigger such a suspension.

Liquidate To close out a position, usually by selling contracts to liquidate a previous long position. See also *Cover.*

Liquid Market A high volume market in which large numbers of contracts may be traded without unduly affecting the market place.

Long A buyer either in the cash market or in the futures market. Usually the buying side of an open futures contract.

Long the Basis A cash market commodity position which is hedged with a sale of futures contracts.

Margin The amount of money which must be deposited with the broker as a guarantee against default. This is analagous to earnest money in a real estate deal.

Margin, Maintenance The minimum amount which must remain in the margin account after any market losses are deducted from the initial margin. Once the account declines to the maintenance level, the broker will request that the client restore the account to its original level. Should the client refuse or default, the position will be closed out by the broker.

Market Order An order to execute a trade as soon as possible at the prevailing market price.

Market If Touched Order A standing order to execute a transaction at a specified price or at one more favorable to the customer. Also called a *Board Order.* Typically used to enter the market.

Maturity Date The date of contract expiration as stated in the commodity contract.

Nearby Delivery   The nearest delivery month in which active trading is taking place. See also *Deferred Delivery*.

Nominal   A price established in very light trading or set as a guideline in the absence of any trading.

Notice Day   A day during the contract delivery month, or on the last business day of the preceeding month, on which a seller may give notice of his intent to deliver.

Offset   To cancel a previous position by making an opposite trade of equal volume, thereby avoiding the delivery process. See also *Cover* and *Liquidate*.

Open Interest   The total number of contracts on one side of the market which have not been offset. If there were 1,000 contracts held by buyers and sellers for a particular delivery month, the open interest would be 500. Since contracts are all in standard volume units, the number of long contracts must equal the number of short contracts.

Open Order   An order which carries from trading day to trading day until it is executed, or until it is cancelled by the original customer.

Open Position   A contract which has not been offset or delivered upon.

Option   Usually a particular delivery month. For example: Instead of saying, "the May contract," traders will sometimes say, "the May option." An option can also refer to Puts and Calls. A Put is an option to sell on or before a specified date at a specified price. A call is an option to buy on or before a specified date at a specified price. Puts and Calls are generally restricted to stocks, although very recently (1972), they have appeared, to a limited extent, in the commodity market.

Overbought   A market price which has been driven too high in relation to the actual conditions of supply and demand.

Oversold A market price which has been driven too low in relation to the actual conditions of supply and demand.

Paper Profit The profit which might have been realized if the contracts had been offset as of a stated date.

Pit The designated location on the floor of the Commodity Exchange where futures market contracts may be traded by exchange members and by open outcry.

Point(s) A point is the smallest nonfractional price unit which is quoted for a commodity. If a commodity is quoted in cents per bushel as $150^1/8$, then one point would be $0.01 per bushel. If a commodity is quoted in dollars per hundredweight as 25.65, then one point would be $0.01 per hundredweight.

Reaction A downward correction of price following an upward trend or leg.

Recovery An upward correction of price following a downward trend or leg.

Resistance A price zone above the current price level which has proven difficult for the market to penetrate. See also *Support*.

Retender An offer to resell or transfer a delivery notice. Buyers may retender notices for most commodities within a specified period of time. If the retender is successful, the new buyer assumes the responsibility of accepting delivery.

Rollover The replacement of one futures market position with another in the same commodity, but in a different delivery month.

Round Trip A futures contract purchase followed by an offsetting sale before delivery, or a sale followed by an offsetting purchase.

Seat A membership in the Commodity Exchange entitling the holder to trade in the pit. Seats are usually sold at public auction to the highest bidder.

Selling Hedge   A long position in the cash market hedged with a short position in the futures market.

Scalper   Floor traders who speculate on small price movements by taking very large positions.

Short   A seller in the cash market or in the futures market. Usually, the selling side of an open futures contract.

Short the Basis   A cash market commodity position which is hedged with a purchase of futures contracts.

Sliding Stop   A Stop Order which is moved up or down with the market until it is executed.

Speculator   A trader who assumes price risk solely in hopes of making a financial profit. He trades commodity futures contracts without owning or ever planning to own the cash commodity represented by those contracts.

Spot Market   The cash commodity market. Actual physical commodity available for delivery.

Spread   The simultaneous purchase of one commodity futures contract(s) and the sale of another contract(s) in a different delivery month, in a different commodity, or traded on a different exchange. The term spread is reserved for operations of this kind involving two grains. See also *Straddle*.

Stop Limit Order   An order directing the broker to buy or sell a specified number of contracts at a stated price or at one more favorable to the customer. The order is not activated until the market price reaches the stated price. Typically used to exit from the market.

Stop Loss Order   A Stop Order used to close out a position which is accumulating a loss.

Stop Order   An order directing the broker to buy or sell a specified number of contracts if the market price reaches a level specified by the customer. The Stop Order becomes a Market Order once the level specified by the customer is reached.

Straddle   The simultaneous purchase of one commodity futures
              contract(s) and the sale of another contract(s)
              in a different delivery month, in a different
              commodity, or traded on a different exchange.
              The term straddle is reserved for operations of
              this kind which do not involve two grains. See
              also *Spread*.

Support   A price zone below the current price level which
              has proven difficult for the market to penetrate
              through. See also *Resistance*.

Technician A trader who relies on price movement patterns to
              decide whether to buy or sell. He generally
              disregards supply and demand conditions.

Thin Market A low volume market in which a large trade unduly
              affects the market price.

Uptick   An upward price movement usually of short
              duration.

Visible Supply The physical volume of a commodity in storage
              at the large terminal markets.

INDEX

A

Account Analysis, 63-65
Afloat, 78
Asked, 78
Average Down, 67,78

B

Bar Chart, 61
Basis:
   defined, 17,78
   description, 14-19,32-33
   example, 21-22,52-54
   movement, 29,57
Bear, 61,78
Bid, 78
Board Order, 37,78
Break, 78
Broker, 78
Bulge, 78
Bull, 61,78
Buying Hedge, 55,58,64
   79

C

Call Point, 79
Carrying Charges:
   defined, 15,79
   example, 21,46,52-54
Clearing House, 11-13,79
Commission, 79
Commodity Exchange, 10,14,26,
   79
Contract:
   defined, 10-11,79
   limits, 31-32
   size, 30
   trading months, 31
   units, 30
Cost, 68-76
Cover, 79

D

Day Order, 37,79
Day Trader, 45
Deferred Delivery, 79
Delivery:
   and speculators, 18,25-26
   example, 53
   mechanism, 11-13,39-40
   month, 79
   notice, 80
   points, 80

E

Exchange Process, 7

F

Financial Leverage, 34-36,46,
   80
Floor Broker, 80
Floor Trader, 80
Fundamental Analysis, 60-61

G

Good Until Cancelled Order,
   37
Grading, 7

H

Hedging:
   defined, 19-23,80
   examples, 41-44,49-53,54-
   58
   month, 36
   volume, 64-66

I

Information Sources, 8,23-24
Inverted Market, 57-58,80

L

Late Tape, 80
Leg, 80
Leverage, 34-36,46,80
Limit Move, 31-32,81
Limit Order, 37
Liquidate, 81
Liquid Market, 81
Loan Security, 47-48
Localized Price, 50,51-52
Long, 39,81
Long The Basis, 81

M

Margin:
  account, 26-27,47-48
  call, 26-27,64
  defined, 26-27,81
  example, 34-36
  loan security, 47-48
  maintenance, 26,81
  short sales, 39
Market If Touched Order, 37, 81
Market Order, 36,38,66,81
Maturity Date, 81
Moving Average, 62-63

N

Nearby Delivery, 82
Nominal Price, 82
Nonstorable Commodities, 32-33
Notice Day, 82

O

Objectives, 47,59
Off At A Specified Time
        Order, 37
Offsetting Trade, 11,25-26, 82
Open Interest, 82
Open Order, 37,82
Open Position, 82
Option, 82

Origin Of The Market, 8
Overbought, 82
Overmargin, 64
Oversold, 83

P

Paper Profit, 83
Pit, 83
Point(s), 83
Position Trader, 45
Price Validation, 44

R

Reaction, 83
Reading Price Reports, 27-32
Recovery, 83
Resistance, 83
Retender, 83
Risk, 7-9,12,19,47
Rollover, 83
Round Trip, 83

S

Scalper, 45,84
Seat, 83
Selling Hedge, 55,58,64,84
Short Selling, 25,38-39,84
Short The Basis, 84
Sliding Stop, 84
Speculator:
  defined, 13,44-47,84
  leverage, 35-36
  producer speculation, 23, 41
  short selling, 25
Spot Market, 84
Spread, 45
Stop Limit Order, 37,84
Stop Loss Order, 37,84
Stop Order, 37,65,84
Stocks, 38-40
Storage, 7
Straddle, 45,85
Support, 85

T

Technical Analysis, 60-63,67
Technician, 85
Thin Market, 85
To Arrive Contracts, 9-10
Trading Rules, 65-67
Trading vs. Investing, 39-40
Transportation, 7-8

U

Uptick, 85

V

Visible Supply, 85

NOTES

NOTES